Teach®
Yourself

# Speed Reading
# In A Week

Tina Konstant

First published in Great Britain in 2012 by Hodder Education

This edition published in 2016 by John Murray Learning

*British Library Cataloguing in Publication Data:* a catalogue record for this title is available from the British Library.

ISBN 9781473609341

eISBN 9781444159486

7

The publisher has used its best endeavours to ensure that any website addresses referred to in this book are correct and active at the time of going to press. However, the publisher and the author have no responsibility for the websites and can make no guarantee that a site will remain live or that the content will remain relevant, decent or appropriate.

The publisher has made every effort to mark as such all words which it believes to be trademarks. The publisher should also like to make it clear that the presence of a word in the book, whether marked or unmarked, in no way affects its legal status as a trademark.

Every reasonable effort has been made by the publisher to trace the copyright holders of material in this book. Any errors or omissions should be notified in writing to the publisher, who will endeavour to rectify the situation for any reprints and future editions.

Typeset by Cenveo® Publisher Services.

Printed and bound in Great Britain by Clays Ltd, Elcograf S.p.A.

John Murray Learning policy is to use papers that are natural, renewable and recyclable products and made from wood grown in sustainable forests. The logging and manufacturing processes are expected to conform to the environmental regulations of the country of origin.

Carmelite House

50 Victoria Embankment

London EC4 0DZ

www.hodder.co.uk

# Contents

# Introduction

When people think about speed reading they often narrow it down to simply reading fast. This, however, is only a small part of the overall process. The key to truly effective speed reading is first being able to identify what you really want or need to read and then reading that carefully selected material – fast.

Take a moment to mentally review all the information that passes in front of you in a typical day: at home, at work, in the papers at the local coffee shop. How much of it do you ignore because it looks like too much to take on, leaving it instead to build up and stack high until you're so behind you need days or weeks to catch up – if you ever manage to at all?

If you had a simple process to follow that allowed you to quickly and easily identify the information you need and eliminate that which you don't need, this backlog of information wouldn't happen and you'd have more time to live your life instead of worrying about what you might be missing because you think you're overloaded.

The aim of this book is to give you the tools you need to get up to date and stay that way.

On Sunday: learn the Five-Step System that will allow you to easily and accurately identify what you must read and what you can ignore, giving you time and energy to pick up a novel or a newspaper on your time off instead of feeling guilty about 'not working'.

On Monday: discover how to increase your reading rate so you can read what you identified as important on Sunday, quickly – except novels which you'll have the time to enjoy at a leisurely pace.

On Tuesday: practise memory techniques which will ensure that you remember what you read when you need it, allowing what you read to become useful and practical instead of short-lived theory.

On Wednesday: understand how your eyes work and prevent eyestrain no matter where or what you read, whether in a book or on a PC.

On Thursday: explore the distractions that slow you down and learn how to prevent them, allowing you to read in any environment – at home, in an open office, on a train.

On Friday: learn how to vary your technique to suit the material you are reading, to ensure that you are able to use the information when and where you need it long after you've read it.

On Saturday: develop your own reading programme to ensure that effective speed reading becomes second nature so you never have to read another book on speed reading!

The key to this book is practice. You don't have to set aside an hour a day, simply use what you learn in this book on everything you read – from books to newspapers and manuals to cornflake boxes. The more you use it, the more natural it will become so, eventually, you'll wonder how you ever read any other way.

SUNDAY

# The five-step system

# In A Week

Tina Konstant

While an undergraduate at the University of Aberdeen, Tina was invited to deliver a series of practical speed-reading workshops to students and the local business community.

She continued to refine and develop the material, which led to speed-reading and information management seminars delivered to businesses in the private and public sectors.

She now consults in the oil and gas sector and writes on a range of subjects from Effective Reading and Information Management to Copywriting and Change Management.

This chapter is the key to effective speed reading. If you only have ten minutes to read one chapter in this book, then make it this one. In it you'll learn a strategy that addresses one of the primary fears people have when it comes to dealing with information: missing something important.

Have you ever been part of a conversation where people are discussing a document or project, only to find that you haven't a clue what they're talking about? Have you ever met people in your field who are talking about new trends that you've never heard of?

The frustration and overload created in situations like this comes from 1) not being able to identify what's relevant and what's not, 2) reading the information but not remembering it and/or 3) not having a strategy for getting through volumes of material in a short amount of time.

This first day outlines a strategy that gives you a solution to these challenges. The skills to identify what you need to read and eliminate what you don't need to read while being certain that you've missed nothing out.

This technique is much like making a good cup of tea; if you follow the instructions, you'll get the result. Only one step of the five-step system needs practice and that step we'll explore in more detail on Monday.

# How to use this book

This book is designed to be a workbook for your speed-reading skills and a reference for you as you practise.

Each day may be referred to independently. This makes it easy for you to locate the information you need. Becoming accustomed to moving freely around a book instead of reading it from front to back is an important habit to develop since most authors don't put the information in precisely the right order to suit *you*.

Which brings us to a most important rule of effective reading: *make your own reading rules*.

Here's a quick guide to reading this book fast and effectively:

1 Flick through the book to get a feel for its structure.
2 Read this chapter carefully so you know and understand how to apply the five-step reading system.
3 Apply the five-step reading system to this book.

As you learn new techniques, practise them here. You will find that you get through the book much faster than you would have imagined and you will have had the opportunity to try out new skills.

# Speed reading raises questions

- What's the fastest possible reading speed?
- How do I remember what I read – when I need to remember it?
- How do I read dry or technical material and maintain concentration?
- Is speed reading easy to learn?

Firstly, we do not know the limit to the speed at which people can read. As an example, Anne Jones read *Harry Potter and the Deathly Hallows* in 47 minutes (4,251 words per minute), then offered to write book reviews for the media to prove her comprehension, comprehension being the most relevant part of the exercise. Why spend precious time reading if you don't plan to remember and perhaps use what you read? Remembering the information long after you have read it, whether fact or fiction, will be explored on Tuesday.

Speed reading is easy. It's the one part of this process that needs some practice but it reflects only one fifth of the reading strategy presented in this book. The rest of the system works simply because you use it.

# The five-step system

There are five stages to the strategy. By the time you complete them you will have:

- explored the material at least three times
- read what you need to have read
- integrated the new knowledge into what you already know
- found the information you need.

And, most importantly, you will have spent a fraction of the time you might otherwise have spent.

To avoid slipping back into old reading habits, accurately follow the five-step process as outlined in this book. Once you are familiar with the system, you can adapt it to any type of reading (articles, newspapers, memos, books or magazines) by combining and omitting steps.

The five-step system has one overriding rule: *always know why you are reading something.*

Whether the reason is 'I want to', 'it looks interesting', or 'because Joe says it'll be a good read' doesn't matter, as long as you have one.

The five steps are:

1 Preparation
2 Structure
3 Language
4 Content
5 Purposeful selection

This system is based on the process of *highlighting* and *eliminating*. As you use the system, your aim is to highlight areas for further study and eliminate those that you are certain you do not need.

Depending on how much you want from the book, steps 1 to 4 could take between five and 40 minutes for a book of 300 pages. The time you spend on step 5 depends on the amount of detailed information you want from the material.

Steps 1 to 5 will now be precisely detailed. Read through this section once, then, using this book or another non-fiction book, try the system out. At this point don't worry about reading fast (as in more 'words per minute') – we'll discuss that tomorrow.

## Step 1: Preparation

One reason that reading can be frustrating is due to a lack of focus and concentration. The preparation stage helps you stay on task.

First:

● Write down what you already know about the subject: key words will be sufficient.

Next:

● Decide what you want from the book – general information, enough information to write a report or simply the answer to a specific question?

Always ask yourself these three questions:

● Why am I reading this in the first place?
● What do I already know?
● What do I need to know?

## Step 2: Structure

The purpose of this stage is to become familiar with the book's *structure*:

● What does it look like?
● Are there summaries or conclusions?
● Is the book all words or are there any pictures?
● What size is the print?
● Is the text broken up into sections?
● Is it a series of paragraphs?

For a 300-page book, this step should take about five minutes.

● *Read* the front and back covers, inside flaps, table of contents, index, and scan the bibliography.
● *Determine* the structure of the book; chapter headings, sub-headings, pictures, graphs, cartoons and images.
● *Eliminate* the parts of the book that you are sure you don't need.

- *Highlight* areas you think you do need.
- *Reaffirm* your decision about what you want from the book.

If it becomes clear that the book does not contain what you need, put it away. You will have saved yourself hours of work.

## Step 3: Language

You have prepared yourself and you know the structure of the book. This next step will familiarize you with the language in the book. Is it full of jargon? Do you need a dictionary even before you begin? Is the language so complex that you decide, at this stage, to get a more basic book on the subject? This step works well if you have completed step 1 (preparation) thoroughly.

A 300-page book should only take between five to ten minutes to review for language.

- Scan the pages at a rate of about a page every few seconds.
- Look for words that stand out and highlight them. They might be names, long or technical words, or words in **bold** or *italics*.
- Study the language: is it technical, non-technical, user-friendly, are you familiar with it?
- Do you need to refer to a dictionary (technical or otherwise) before you carry on?

The bonus of going through this step is that as well as getting familiar with the language, you'll also pick up some of the key ideas, putting you in good shape for step four.

### An important note

If you know *why* you are reading the book you will know *what* you are looking for and words related to your area of interest will stand out. Try this now: look around the room for everything red. Only red. Notice how much and how many shades of red there are in the room. Now, close your eyes and try and remember everything blue in the room ... what did you notice? If you know what you are looking for, you will find it.

## Step 4: Content

This is the first time you will be doing anything close to reading. Most well-written material will outline the aim or core of each chapter in the first paragraph and the contents of each paragraph will be made clear in the first sentence of that paragraph. So, for more detail:

● read the first paragraph of every chapter; and
● the first sentence of every paragraph (and the last if the paragraph is very long).

As you read – cross out, highlight, underline, circle, take notes and mind-map. The more thoroughly you do this, the more effective the final stage will be.

## Step 5: Purposeful selection

Here is a thought experiment (don't actually do this unless you want to fall foul of mountain rescue).

Imagine you are to take a trip from London to Edinburgh. You are to use country roads as far as possible. Imagine you have never taken such a trip before, but still you decide not to use a map. On your arrival in Edinburgh, check your time, which will include all the detours you had to take and the stops you had to make to ask for directions. Make the trip a second time with a map, then compare the ease and speed of the two journeys.

The same principle applies to reading. Steps 1 to 4 create a map for you to follow. Once you know where you are going and how you are going to get there, the task is much easier to accomplish.

The aim of the first four steps is to allow you to select what you need or want to read with purpose.

During the first four steps you have decided what it is you want to read, what answers you are looking for and what you are interested in about the subject. You have studied the structure of the book, you are familiar with the language, you have read approximately one third of the content and you have an excellent understanding of what information the book contains. You are now in a position to select the sections you really need to read without worrying whether you have missed anything out or not.

To do this most effectively:

● Review the notes you made in step 1.
● Add to your notes any information you have gained as you have been reading.
● Ask: 'Have I found what I'm looking for?'
● If you have what you need, stop.
● If not, review the key words you have highlighted in step 3 and repeat the question: 'Do I have what I want yet?'
● You made notes in step 4: review them and again ask whether you have what you want.
● If you decide that you need more information, then go through the book and read the sections you identified as relevant during the first four steps.
● If you do decide you need to read the entire book you will find you will be able to read it much faster, because, having completed the first four steps, you will know what the book contains and what to expect.

 *If you know nothing about a subject it is almost impossible to remember what you read. The five-step system helps you build a framework of knowledge, making retention and recall easier.*

# Summary

SUNDAY

MONDAY

TUESDAY

WEDNESDAY

THURSDAY

FRIDAY

SATURDAY

By the time you've applied the five-step system to any non-fiction material, you will be familiar with the layout, the key ideas in the book, the language and a good deal of the content. By step 4 of the five-step system you will have been able to delete sections that have no relevance and highlight areas that you need to study in more depth (step 5).

How much more time you spend on the material will depend on exactly what you want from it. It might be that you've identified the page and paragraph that contain the answer to your question, or you might have decided that you still need to read it all. Whatever you choose, it will be an informed decision and you'll be spending your time reading material you are sure you want to read.

The best way to learn anything new is to use it. Take a few minutes to apply the five-step system to this book. Review the steps and give yourself a target of 20 minutes to get as much as you can from the book. Once you've identified the sections of the book you want to focus on, then read those using the speed-reading techniques outlined on Monday.

# Questions

1. What is the fastest possible reading speed?
   a) 500 words per minute ❏
   b) 1000 words per minute ❏
   c) 25,000 words per minute ❏
   d) Who knows? We're learning more about what the human brain can do every day! Our only limits are the ones we place on ourselves. ❏

2. Is speed reading easy to learn?
   a) No – it takes a lot of practice. ❏
   b) Yes – after hours of practice. ❏
   c) Yes – if you have Einstein's IQ. ❏
   d) Yes – if you apply these techniques to anything you read. ❏

3. The purpose of reviewing the structure of a book is to:
   a) get an overview of the book. ❏
   b) eliminate parts of the book you are sure you don't need. ❏
   c) highlight areas you think you might need. ❏
   d) All of the above. ❏

4. What is the overriding rule of the five-step system?
   a) Always know why you're reading something. ❏
   b) Always wear rubber-soled shoes in a thunderstorm. ❏
   c) Whenever you read anything boring, have plenty of strong coffee to hand. ❏
   d) If you're going to read anything after midnight, do 50 press-ups first. ❏

5. What should you do if you discover (in step 2) that the book won't give you the information you need?
   a) Finish the book because you've started it. ❏
   b) Put down the book and move onto something else – you've saved yourself hours of work. ❏
   c) Put down the book until later, then review it again. ❏
   d) Redo the five-step process in case you've missed something. ❏

6. During the 'language' stage, what are you looking for?
   a) Jargon ❏
   b) Unfamiliar terminology ❏
   c) Any words or phrases you don't understand ❏
   d) All of the above ❏

7. What is the greatest challenge you'll face in step 4?
   a) Pulled eye muscles ❏
   b) Flea bites ❏
   c) Being trapped in old habits and reading more than the first sentence and first paragraph of every section ❏
   d) Falling asleep ❏

8. By the time you've completed steps 1 to 4, you'll have read approximately:
   a) 90% of the book ❏
   b) 10% of the book ❏
   c) 33.3% of the book ❏
   d) None of the book ❏

9. Why is it important to know why you're reading something?
a) It's easy to find what you're looking for when you know what it is. ❏
b) It saves time. ❏
c) It gives you focus and motivation. ❏
d) All of the above. ❏

10. How does the five-step system improve memory?
a) It builds a framework of knowledge. ❏
b) By the time you get to step 5, you've gone through the information four times and repetition aides recall. ❏
c) The five-step system increases your reading rate, which helps keep you alert. ❏
d) All of the above. ❏

SUNDAY

MONDAY

TUESDAY

WEDNESDAY

THURSDAY

FRIDAY

SATURDAY

# MONDAY

## Speed reading

There are a number of factors that will influence the speed at which you can read, and these are covered in this chapter, followed by speed-reading techniques that will help you through any challenges you might face.

The key to success in this chapter is to enjoy it. If you allow yourself to get frustrated and uptight, then no amount of practice will increase your reading rate. Instead, follow the instructions through steps 1 to 4 of the five-step system; when you reach step 5, you will have a vastly reduced amount to read. You can then choose how fast you want to read based on the type of material, its complexity, how much detail you need and how much time you have.

If you're under too much pressure, you're likely to go mentally blank and won't be able to read at all. Relax, breathe and read at the most appropriate speed for the material and what you want from it.

The more you read, the better you will get at recognizing when to read fast and when to slow down. The more flexible you are with your reading, the faster the overall session will go and the more you'll retain. The good news is that this is the only part of the five-step reading process that needs practice.

SUNDAY

MONDAY

TUESDAY

WEDNESDAY

THURSDAY

FRIDAY

SATURDAY

The more you read the better you will become at recognizing when you can read fast and when to slow down.

# Factors contributing to speed

Factors contributing to the speed at which you can read are:

- **Familiarity with the subject-related terminology** – if you are already familiar with the subject you will already have a framework on which to build and you will be able to read quite quickly because you will not have to stop to think about what key words mean and how the ideas fit together.
- **Clarity of purpose** – remember step 1 of the five-step system. The clearer your purpose is, the faster you will be able to read. Always know why you are reading something.
- **The difficulty of the text** – some material is difficult to read even if you are familiar with the terminology and content – this includes anything technical or industry specific like legal or medical texts.
- **Urgency and stress levels** – have you ever noticed that when you absolutely have to read something immediately you find that you can't read it fast? Stress will slow you down. On Tuesday, stress will be considered in conjunction with concentration and memory.

- **Mood** – if you are feeling tired, restless, impatient or irritable, you may find that you will be unable to read as fast as when you feel alert, fresh, happy and relaxed. You may not always be alert, fresh, happy and relaxed when you have to read so, if you can, learn how to manage your feelings so that you can concentrate regardless of how you might be feeling at the time.

# What you need to improve speed

Many of us are taught that in order to be fully informed we need to read every word in the book or article we've chosen. But in reality, with so much information available to us, it makes more sense to select what we need at the time and leave the rest. The first four steps of this system will help you with that selection process giving you the time and mental focus to speed-read the relevant content.

To improve your reading speed you will need:

- good background knowledge of the subject or, if you do not have that yet, a strategy for building the background knowledge quickly
- familiarity with the language related to the subject
- a good vocabulary
- a desire to learn how to improve your reading
- a good attitude towards reading – ask yourself the question: 'What is it that I get from speed reading?'
- practise – if you use these techniques every day you will find that the speed at which you read, your recall, comprehension and the flexibility of your reading will quickly improve.

# Increasing your basic reading rate

The main reason that we tend to read slowly is because we read with our ears instead of with our eyes (more about this on

Wednesday). The second reason we read slowly is because we are easily distracted by what's on the page and by what's going on around us.

# Using a pacer

A pacer is a tool that will help you to eliminate most of your speed-reading problems. A pacer can be your finger, a chopstick, a pencil or pen, or even speed-reading software.

A pacer helps to eliminate most distractions, and it includes an extra sense (touch) in the reading process. Using a pacer adds a kinaesthetic, physical dimension to your reading. You are actually *doing* something instead of simply reading. You are involving your hands as well.

Using a pacer helps your reading in several ways.

- It increases your reading rate by encouraging your eyes to focus on more than one word at a time.
- The pacer focuses you on what you are reading instead of allowing your eyes to jump around the page at anything that attracts your attention.

Here is an experiment for you to try. Find someone willing to take part. Ask that person to draw a circle in the air using their eyes. Notice the eye movements – are they smooth or jerky? Do they create a full circle or does it look like they are making corners? Next, ask them to draw a circle in the air with their finger and this time to follow their finger with their eyes. Watch their eyes. Do you notice that the second time their eyes move smoothly, quickly and deliberately?

The pacer also

- helps you move to new lines smoothly and easily
- prevents you losing your place
- prevents sub-vocalization (the voice inside your head caused by reading with your ears) by speeding up the pace at which you read and allowing you to see more than one word at a time.

## How to use a pacer

You can use a pen, a chopstick, a finger, anything you like, as a pacer. To begin, place your pacer on the first word on the line and move it smoothly across the page or screen to the end of the line, then return it to the next line.

Use your pacer to read the next paragraph. Place the pacer on the dotted line and move it smoothly across the line. Re-read the paragraph several times until you feel that you have the rhythm smooth and fast – also, move the pacer just a little bit more quickly than you think you can 'read'.

It is important that the pacer moves smoothly and steadily across the page. If the movement is hesitant your eyes are dictating the pace at which you read and your reading rate will not increase. If the pacer moves smoothly, your eyes, with practice, will learn to keep up and your brain will learn to absorb the meaning of words in a new way.

What was different about reading with a pacer? How did you feel? How much faster did you feel you read? How do you feel about comprehension?

Are you still reading with your pacer? For the duration of this book read using a pacer. By the time you finish the book you will find that it has become second nature and you will be well on the way to becoming an expert speed-reader.

# Different types of pacing

The pacing you are using now is one basic method for guiding your eye across the page. There are different methods of pacing for different types of material and different readers' needs.

## Technical material with which you are not familiar

Place the pacer under every line and move it steadily across the page from the beginning to the end of each line. This method ensures that you miss nothing.

## Technical material with which you are familiar

Place your pacer under every second line. This method encourages you to read more than one line at a time and ultimately to understand the meaning much more quickly.

## Material with which you are very familiar

If you are very familiar with the material and you only need to have a general idea about what you are reading you can run the pacer down either the side or the middle of the page.

Ultimately, the more you experiment and the more flexible your reading becomes, the easier you will find it to change from one technique to another.

---

**Practice box**
Novels are the best source of practice to develop flexibility in pacing. At the start of the novel you might find that you pace under every line, then as you get familiar with the plot you might pace under every two lines. When the story really gets going and you are looking for the exciting bits in between the description, you

---

might find that you run the pacer down the middle of the page until you find the sections of the book that really carry the story. Your enjoyment of the book is not lessened in any way at all – in fact you might find that you actually finish more novels than you used to.

Hints to increase your speed:

- **Push yourself quite hard.** It is easy to stay in the comfort zone of reading slowly. Once you break through the barrier of believing that you can only remember what you read when you hear every word, your enjoyment of reading and your pace will increase.
- **Practise – often.** Use everything you read as a practice medium. Speed-read the instructions on the back of a bottle or the sales blurb on the back of a cereal packet. Instead of just reading as you have previously, read with the purpose of going as fast as you can for good comprehension. Use a pacer when you do so.
- **Build the context first.** The first four steps of the five-step system will make speed reading anything easy and several times faster than if you were reading it for the first time.
- **The faster you go the less you will vocalize.** Later on today, we will discuss ways of building speed and maintaining it – play with these exercises daily until you feel that they are a natural part of your reading strategy.
- **Eliminate or decrease distractions.** On Thursday, we look at different distractions you are likely to encounter and some solutions to them. The more you are able to concentrate, the faster you will be able to read.
- **Read actively.** Take notes, mark and highlight relevant sections, make comments as you read, build reading maps and think about the arguments as you read. If you must do any talking inside your head while you read, choose to make it a debate or dialogue on aspects of the topic with the author. The more actively you read, the better your understanding and long-term comprehension will be.

It is important to remember that speed reading is not about reading fast all the time. The technical content of the material, the print size, your familiarity with the subject, and, particularly, your purpose for reading can affect the speed at which you read. The key to speed reading is having the choice to read as fast or as slow as you wish.

# Skimming and scanning
## What is the difference?

The difference between skimming and scanning is that when you scan for information you stop once you have it. With skimming you don't stop, unless you want to.

## When are they used?

Scanning is used when you are looking for specific information; an answer to a particular question or a telephone number in a directory.

Skimming is used during step 3 of the five-step system. You use skimming when you know what you are looking for and want a general impression of what the text contains.

There are different types of skimming depending on what your purpose is:

- **Skimming to overview** – the purpose of this method is to get an outline of what the document is about. You will be looking more at structure than at content. This method is used mostly in the second step of the five-step system.
- **Skimming to preview** – this is when you know you are going to re-read the material. Your purpose is to gather as much background information as you can on the subject without spending too much time on it.
- **Skimming to review** – you would use this method when you have already read the material and your purpose is just to refamiliarize yourself with the content.

## Successful skimming

Skimming for information is easier when you know where the information is likely to be within the overall scheme of the piece you are reading. While you are speed reading, look for the core information. Once you have stated your purpose for skimming and you know what you are looking for, you will be able to identify trigger words that hold the relevant information:

- who
- what
- where
- why
- when
- how.

Other key words are those that distinguish fact from opinion. An author might spend the first half of a paragraph giving fact, then you may find words like:

- but
- nonetheless
- however
- yet
- on the other hand.

These key words signify that the author may be drifting from fact to opinion. If you are looking for an author's opinion on a subject, look for these words.

---

**Practice box**
Practise this by going through newspaper or magazine articles with the purpose of identifying the *who*, *what*, *where*, *why*, *when* and *how*, as well as the author's opinions, as quickly as you can.

---

# Getting the message

When you read, you convert the information embedded in groups of words into ideas, images, thoughts, feelings and actions. One of the purposes of reading is getting the message that the words carry. This does not necessarily mean that you have to read all the words. When you speed-read – especially when you start to get used to reading more than one line at a time – you might at first get confused because the words may be presented to you in a different order to the one that was intended. When you read with your eyes, you will find, however, that this does not present a problem because your brain works out what the sentence means regardless of what order the words are in.

Your brain is always trying to make sense of information it receives. When the information you are reading is not complete your brain will naturally fill in the blanks and organize the information so that you can make sense of it. First, read the following sentences out loud and work out what they mean:

*We'll 20 minutes in be there.*
*Let's dinner for tonight go out.*
*Reading visual activity done slowly is only the.*

Now, look at the next batch of sentences and get the meaning from them as quickly as you can by looking at the whole sentence and identifying the key words:

*Speed reading have if you a purpose is easy.*
*Have yet holiday you been on this year?*
*The improve is to best way to practise.*

Which was quicker – reading with your ears or reading with your eyes?

You don't have to have the words in the right order to get the message.

# 'It's all in the words' – developing a good vocabulary

The bigger your vocabulary, the faster you will be able to read. Hesitating at words you are unfamiliar with wastes time. Unfamiliar terminology makes you think about the whole passage, not just the word. Several questions might go through your head. What does this word mean? Does it change the context? Is it important to my understanding of the text? These questions go through your mind very quickly, but the problem is that once you have answered them you may have forgotten what you have been reading. The real time-waster is when you have to return to the beginning of a passage and start again.

Solving the vocabulary problem is relatively easy. Some vocabulary will become clear to you within the context of the paragraph; the rest you should look up before you begin step 5.

> **During steps 3 and 4 of the five-step system look for unfamiliar words as part of the skimming exercise, then look them up before you begin step 5.**

Ways of increasing your vocabulary:

- Pay attention to new words.
- Keep a small notebook where you write down new terminology (with meanings) that you come across in reading and in conversation.
- Use your new vocabulary.
- Become familiar with the roots of words. If you understand the root, you will be able to work out the meaning of many words. All good dictionaries will show you the roots.

# Reading exercises

Here are some exercises to increase your speed-reading rate.

## Stretching speed and comprehension

This quick exercise will help improve your memory and increase your speed.

1 Using a pacer, read one page as fast as you can.
2 Stop and write down everything you can remember.
3 Read five pages like this every day, gradually increasing the number of pages you read before you stop to recall what you read.

4 Start with a familiar subject, then, as your ability, confidence and comfort become more apparent to you, move on to more challenging material.

## Stretching speed – the one-minute trip

1 Read for one minute and count how many lines you have read.
2 Continue reading for another minute, reading two lines more than you did the first time.
3 In the next minute, read four lines more than you did before, then six, then eight, then ten.
4 Always read for good comprehension and recall. As soon as you feel you are not understanding or remembering the text, consolidate at that level until you are comfortable. Then speed up again gradually.

Reading quickly requires concentration. If you don't understand or remember what you read you may find your concentration drifting because you are becoming disappointed and perhaps bored.

As your concentration improves, stretch the one-minute trip to two minutes, then four minutes, then six, and eight ... and so on.

## Mostly reading

This technique is good for the parts of the text with which you are already fairly familiar and when you want to be sure you have missed nothing out.

1 Read the *first* sentence of the paragraph.
2 Skim the rest of the paragraph for key words and, if necessary, read the *last* sentence of the paragraph.

## Metronome pacing

You can buy a small electronic metronome at any music shop quite cheaply – it will be a good investment.

Do this exercise for two minutes, then relax for five minutes.

1 Set the metronome at its slowest speed and read one line per 'tick'.
2 Every page or half page increase the pace of the metronome by one, or by as much as you are comfortable with, until you reach the fastest speed on the metronome.
3 Then relax.

The metronome will reach a speed at which you will not be able to read every word. This exercise 'pushes' your eye and brain to see and absorb more than one word at a time, and gradually stretches your ability.

If you drive on a motorway at 70 miles per hour and, as you approach a town, you suddenly have to reduce your speed to 30, you might slow down and think you are travelling at 30 until the police stop you and inform you that you were travelling at 40 or 50 – much faster than you thought.

The similarity between driving and speed reading doesn't stop there. Travelling at 70 miles an hour you have to concentrate and don't have time to look at the scenery. When speed reading you are reading so fast that your mind doesn't want to wander as much as it can at '30 miles per hour'.

# Summary

Most habits are subconscious, so they're pretty hard to fix. The first step to changing a habit is working out you have it and admitting to it!

The challenge with learning to speed-read is that your new reading habits will compete with old habits that you've been enforcing every day since you learned to read. As a result, reading fast is the only part of the five-step system that will take a bit of time to get used to and practice to get right.

The key is to reduce vocalizing and sub-vocalizing.

- To stop yourself vocalizing (mouthing the words), put a pencil between your teeth while you read. You'll soon notice if you start moving your lips.
- With sub-vocalizing (saying the words in your mind), the faster you read, the less you'll sub-vocalize.

Be patient – you've been reading to yourself for many years and your memory strategies are well established. The more you practise, the easier it'll get. Make the job easier by focusing on the first four steps of the five-step system and reducing the amount of unnecessary information as much as possible. Then take the time to practise speed reading techniques on the remaining material knowing that if you need to, you can slow down and you'll still have read the book faster than you would have previously.

SUNDAY
MONDAY
TUESDAY
WEDNESDAY
THURSDAY
FRIDAY
SATURDAY

# Questions

1. What factor(s) can help increase your reading rate?
   a) Familiarity with the subject ❏
   b) Clarity of purpose ❏
   c) Mood ❏
   d) All of the above ❏

2. What do you need to increase your reading rate?
   a) A 21-speed bike ❏
   b) Someone standing over your shoulder ❏
   c) Focus and attention ❏
   d) A lot of caffeine ❏

3. What should you use as a pacer?
   a) Your finger ❏
   b) Anything as long as it works ❏
   c) A pen ❏
   d) A chopstick ❏

4. A pacer will help you:
   a) move to new lines easily ❏
   b) keep you eyes on the page ❏
   c) prevent excessive sub-vocalization. ❏
   d) All of the above. ❏

5. Speed reading needs practice because:
   a) you're working on breaking an old and engrained habit. ❏
   b) anything new needs practice. ❏
   c) it's difficult. ❏
   d) it seems like something that'll be fun to do on a Saturday night. ❏

6. What is skimming?
   a) A technique to use when you know what you want and just want a general overall impression of the material. ❏
   b) Bouncing rocks over water. ❏
   c) Taking the best bits off the top of a chocolate pudding. ❏
   d) All of the above. ❏

7. What is scanning?
   a) Finding specific information like a phone number or the answer to a particular question. ❏
   b) Digitizing a document. ❏
   c) Running your eyes across a view looking for something specific. ❏
   d) All of the above. ❏

8. Why is developing a good vocabulary useful?
   a) It's fun to confuse your friends. ❏
   b) Fancy words make you seem smart. ❏
   c) The easier it is to recognize new words, the faster you'll read them. ❏
   d) If no one else understands what you're saying, they won't ask questions you can't answer. ❏

9. What is sub-vocalizing?
   a) Saying the words in your head while you read. ❏
   b) An underground train. ❏
   c) Noises rabbits make in their burrows. ❏
   d) The language you use when you're telling your boss where to go. ❏

10. What might be the best way to stop you moving your lips while you read?
a) Putting a pencil between your teeth ❏
b) Taping your mouth shut ❏
c) Have someone tug your ears every time you do it ❏
d) Any of the above, as long as it works ❏

SUNDAY
MONDAY
TUESDAY
WEDNESDAY
THURSDAY
FRIDAY
SATURDAY

# TUESDAY

## Remember what you read

The most common complaint people have about reading – fast or slow – is their ability to remember what they read. This concern isn't linked just to remembering something a week, month or year later, but ten seconds later!

Have you ever got to the end of a paragraph or page and had to go back to the beginning because you can't recall anything you've read? Even worse, have you ever studied for an exam and gone back to revise only to realize you don't even recall seeing the page (despite your handwritten notes all over it), let alone remember the content? Memory is fickle. There are all sorts of physical, mental and environmental distractions that can contribute to you forgetting something as soon as you've looked at it.

Conversely, you might read an odd and interesting fact that has no relevance at the time, but you'll remember it forever.

We'll probably never fully understand human memory, what we're capable of and how to tap into it to get more consistent results, but there are certainly a few strategies we can employ to help ensure that when we read (with purpose in mind) our chances of remembering are greatly improved.

The key to all these memory techniques is to follow the primary rule of the five-step system: have a clear purpose. With that in mind, today we'll look at the memory process, how it works and how to get the best from it.

SUNDAY MONDAY TUESDAY WEDNESDAY THURSDAY FRIDAY SATURDAY

# Memory myths

There is the danger that modern living is overloading the human memory system. There is much more for us to remember than there was for our grandparents. With mass communication growing, more paper being printed than ever before and the emphasis of success moving from physical strength to mental power, we have to develop skills that help us keep up before we can get ahead. The main factor contributing to this overload, however, is not necessarily the amount of information we are faced with but rather our *attitude* towards it.

> **TIP** *When faced with a huge amount of information, the real damage is done by the stress it induces rather than the data itself. So when you're faced with an overload of information, deal first with your attitude. Calm down, relax, get some perspective, then apply the five-step system. If you're not careful, stress will creep up and cripple you before you start.*

Normally, we're only aware of our memories when we forget something. It's a big issue for reading because most people find remembering what they want to remember when they read challenging. This is mainly because they are not using an appropriate method for retaining the text.

There are some myths and false assumptions about memory that need to be countered first.

- Memory is *not* a stand-alone system. It relies on perception, attention and reasoning. Each of these areas will be discussed further today.
- Memory is *not* a system that is based on isolated facts.
- Everything you remember *is connected* to other pieces of information in your memory.
- Memory retrieval relies greatly on *association*. The more connected your memories are, the easier it will be to recall information.
- New information is *not* stored separately from old information. Old knowledge helps make sense of new

information and vice versa. That is one reason why it is easier to read material you know something about.

● Memory is *not only* designed to store information; it is also designed to *use* it.
● We speak about memory as if it is an *object*. We tend to describe ourselves as having a good, bad or average memory, just like having good or bad lungs. But your memory is not a *thing*. It is certainly not a *single* thing. It's a series of processes that take place throughout your brain, *all the time.*
● Your memory *can* be trained. It has been said that there are no good or bad memories, just trained or untrained. With very few exceptions, and barring organic damage, everyone is born with a memory that can be developed.

The more you use your memory, the stronger it will get. Many of the problems people have with their memories when they grow older are due to lack of mental exercise, lack of physical exercise, poor nutrition, excess stress and/or poor coping strategies.

The basic guideline for improving your memory and ability to concentrate by focusing on physical and mental health is that what is good for the body is also good for the mind.

# How memory works – and when it doesn't

There are many models for how the memory system works. Basically, your memory is divided into three functions:

● acquisition – absorbing information
● retention – keeping it in your head
● retrieval – getting it out again.

A memory can become unavailable at any point. The trouble is that you only know it is unavailable when you try to retrieve it: you are standing in front of a person whose name you have forgotten, trying to introduce him to someone else whose name you have also forgotten.

There are some basic memory rules to follow at each phase to help you remember.

# Memory acquisition

*The first rule of acquisition is pay attention.* Most of the time we 'forget' something because we didn't have the opportunity to remember it in the first place. Have you ever been told someone's name only to realize two seconds later that you have 'forgotten' it? Chances are your attention was elsewhere. The same phenomenon occurs when you read.

If you have internal talk going on inside your head, asking yourself whether you are likely to remember what you are reading or not, the chances are you will not remember much at all.

*The second rule of acquisition is plan.* Before you begin, think of when you are likely to use the information you are reading. Then, decide which memory tool (to be discussed later on today) will help best when the time comes to use the information in the future.

*The third rule of acquisition is be interested.* Even if the material seems dull, find something in it that interests you. If you are bored, then parts of your brain will go to sleep and you will find paying attention even more difficult.

*The final rule of acquisition is be active.* Read actively. Think about what you read. When you follow the five-step system and you *prepare* to read, take some time to think about what you already know on the subject. As we saw from the 'myths and assumptions', your memory does not work in isolation. The more connections you make between the new and old information the easier it will be to understand what you are reading. Understanding is the key to remembering.

# Memory retention

Keeping information in your head is one thing, keeping it there in such a way that you can retrieve it later is a different matter.

Your memory thrives on association. The better connected your memory is the easier it will be to retrieve information when you need it. Also, you don't have to keep everything in your head. You can be just as connected on paper as long as you know where to find the information when you need it.

These simple memory tools will help you organize your reading so that retrieval is easy.

## Memory retrieval

One reason we have difficulty retrieving information is that we use the wrong method of retrieval. Memories are stored in several parts of your brain. When you try to remember what your front door looks like several areas of your brain will be activated. You might:

- see an internal picture of what your door looks like (visual)
- hear the sound of it closing (auditory)
- recall the last time you walked in or out (kinaesthetic and proprioceptive)
- remember the feeling of the last time you locked yourself out (emotional)
- smell the fresh coat of paint from when you painted it last (olfactory).

When we try to retrieve information we often use only one access point. If you can recreate the whole experience as you remember it, you will be able to recall it more easily.

## The importance of concentration

Without concentration there is no memory. Remember the first rule of acquisition – pay attention. Ideas on how to concentrate and avoid the distractions that break up your concentration will be discussed on Thursday.

Concentration does not come easily to many people for two reasons:

- We are very easily distracted.
- There is much to distract us.

Improving concentration isn't always easy. We don't always have the time or the desire to meditate and practise absolute concentration for several hours each day. Fortunately, there are other ways of getting results.

# Improving concentration

## Interest and motivation

The more you are interested in what you are doing, the easier it is to concentrate. Remember the last time you were so engrossed in what you were doing that you lost all count of time. Nothing else distracted your attention. You were totally interested and motivated towards a goal. There are two words to take particular note of – motivated and goal.

When you know what you are after (a goal) and why you are doing it (motivated) then the desire (interest) to complete the task successfully makes for total concentration.

However, if the job is particularly boring and it is hard to find either motivation or interest, then make the *process of reading* the challenge. Make a decision that, for example:

- Your *goal* is to finish this task as quickly as possible.
- Your *motivation* is that you can get home sooner or get on with another more interesting task.
- Your *interest* is developing a system that will allow you to get through boring material faster and more effectively every time you are faced with it.

## Mental numbers

You will be surprised at how easily you can be distracted without realizing it is happening. Try this simple experiment: count from one to 26. Notice at what number another thought comes into your head.

Many people will have another thought in their minds by the time they reach five. When you count, it is easy to think of other things and still keep going because counting from one to 26 is a simple exercise. When you are reading, the mental energy needed to focus your attention increases and these drifting thoughts contribute to lack of concentration.

You might like to use the following experiment to increase your concentration.

Simultaneously count from one to 26 and go through the alphabet from A to Z, thus: 1 – A – 2 – B – 3 – C – 4 – D – 5 – E ... and so on. Imagine the numbers on the left side of your brain and the letters on the right side. Then switch sides, imagine the numbers on the right side of your brain and the letters on the left.

How fast you can go? How far can you go before you realize your attention has drifted? Once you can go through the alphabet and up to 26 fluently going forwards, try it backwards.

When you feel that your concentration is dipping, do the exercise a few times. It can be quite meditative and relaxing.

# Techniques for remembering what you read

There are many ways to remember what you read. Some are listed below. The aim is to be comfortable with all of them and be able to use the right one for the material you are reading. Everyone is different, so experiment with all the approaches.

## Linear

Make notes as you read or after each section. These should include your own thoughts, ideas and cross-references. The more you include your own ideas the stronger your long-term memory will be.

## Key words

Highlight the words that carry the message. If you do make notes separately, ensure that the key words are correct, so as to avoid having a list of words that make no sense to you when you review the information in the future.

## Margin reading

Many people are brought up to believe that books are to be kept in perfect condition. However, a book is just a form of communication from the author to the reader. You start to take ownership of a book by writing in it or marking it. Underline, circle, highlight essential areas, note your opinions, whether you agree or disagree, and mark what you do or don't understand, and do something about that 'not understanding'. This should only be done if the book belongs to you and is not a priceless antique!

## Mind-mapping

● Place the key idea in the centre of a horizontal (landscape) page.
● Main ideas form thick branches from the centre.
● Secondary ideas flow from the main ideas.
● Tertiary ideas flow from the secondary ideas.
● And so on until you reach the finest relevant detail.
● Use colours and symbols.
● Use one word or idea per line.

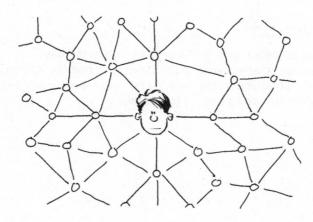

## Multi-sensory reading

Do you remember your front door? Do you remember what it sounds like when you close it? What does fresh paint smell like? What does it feel like to be locked out? What colour is it? Multi-sensory reading uses as many of your senses as possible to help you make sense of and absorb the information. Here are some ideas on how to involve your other senses while you read:

- **Sight** – imagine what you are reading in your mind; create a film of the story you are being told.
- **Hearing** – speak to people about the subject; ask questions as you read, teach someone else, make up rhymes and stories.
- **Touch** – draw pictures and symbols representing the information. If the information is something you can do – do it instead of just reading about it.

The more senses you involve in learning new information the easier it will be to recall it because the information will be accessible via more than one function of your brain.

The five-step system and memory techniques work if you simply use them. The more you practise and the more you become aware of memory, the better you will become.

# Revision

A basic guideline is to revise seven times in ten days. To remember what you read in the long term, use the information. As mentioned under 'Memory myths', the memory process is designed for use as well as for storage.

# Summary

Like many deeply held beliefs, a lot of what we believe about memory is based on myth and old information that makes sense on the surface but doesn't really stand up to serious investigation.

We use those beliefs to explain faults in our capacity to remember, which is why people say, 'I have a hopeless memory for names/faces/ numbers/facts/figures/what I read ...' – take your pick – and everyone nods and agrees that they have the same issue.

The truth is, if we have these 'issues', we're either not applying ourselves to the task of improving our memory in that particular area, or we're not interested in names/faces/numbers/ facts/figures/what we read ...

If there is any type of information that you seem to magically absorb, no matter what format it's in or what the environment in which you read it, then you'll know that your memory works fine.

Take time to consider why some information is easy to remember. You'll probably find that you're interested, or think it will be useful to you personally.

If you could find a degree of interest or usefulness in the information you struggle to absorb, you'll find that your ability to retain and recall that information will increase exponentially.

Having a purpose and applying the five-step system to such material (knowing why you're reading something and when you'll use it) will go a long way to helping you.

SUNDAY
MONDAY
TUESDAY
WEDNESDAY
THURSDAY
FRIDAY
SATURDAY

# Questions

1. Why do we struggle with our memories so much?
a) Too much information ❏
b) Too little time ❏
c) Not enough focus ❏
d) All of the above ❏

2. What myths and assumptions do we make about our memories?
a) It's a standalone system. ❏
b) New information is stored separately from old information. ❏
c) Memory can't be trained. ❏
d) All of the above. ❏

3. What are the general elements of our memory process?
a) Remember, forget, give up ❏
b) Acquisition, retention, retrieval ❏
c) Try to remember, fail hopelessly, pretend we know people we don't ❏
d) All of the above ❏

4. The rules of memory acquisition are:
a) try, try harder, try again. ❏
b) pay attention, plan, be interested, be active. ❏
c) listen once, give up, don't bother again. ❏
d) cry. ❏

5. Why is concentration so important when you read?
a) There's no memory without it. ❏
b) The better you focus, the faster you'll read. ❏

c) It allows you to get through your in-tray faster. ❏
d) All of the above. ❏

6. Which of the following techniques will help you remember what you read?
a) Highlighting key words ❏
b) Mind-mapping ❏
c) Multi-sensory reading ❏
d) All of the above ❏

7. Multi-sensory reading is:
a) reading using all your senses. ❏
b) reading actively. ❏
c) being engaged. ❏
d) questioning the author. ❏

8. Basic guidelines for frequency of revision are:
a) read it once a day for the rest of your life. ❏
b) read it once and only once. ❏
c) read it seven times in ten days. ❏
d) read it five minutes before you need the information. ❏

9. Why can concentrating be so challenging?
a) We're easily distracted. ❏
b) There's a lot to distract us. ❏
c) When it comes to work, we're probably not that interested in most of what we have to read. ❏
d) All of the above. ❏

**10.** When are we most aware of our memory challenges?

a) When we forget something. ❑

b) When we're talking to someone who seems to know everything about us but whose face we don't recognize. ❑

c) When the word we need is right there, on the tip of our tongue, but just won't come out. ❑

d) All of the above and a whole lot more. ❑

# WEDNESDAY

## Your eyes and effective reading

The most important tools you have for reading are your eyes. Any discomfort or strain will affect concentration immediately. When you are tired, or if the lighting is wrong, you are likely to experience discomfort in your eyes. If your eyes hurt, a headache may follow quickly. Soon, you may find you have lost concentration and it is difficult to read. It is easier to look after your eyes continually, than it is to have to treat them when something goes wrong owing to bad habits.

The exercises in this chapter will give you an idea of what your eyes do while you read.

# How the eyes work when you read
## Speed-reading basics

The main reason people read at an average reading rate of 150–250 words per minute is because that is approximately the rate at which people speak.

While you are reading this paragraph listen to what is going on inside your head. Do you hear a voice inside your head while you are reading? Are you saying the words inside your mind while you read? This happens because of the way most people are *taught* how to read.

When we are first taught to read we learn to recognize one letter or sound at a time; then, when we have mastered that we move on to recognizing one word at a time. The next step is being able to read out loud so that your teacher can see that you have learned to recognize the words accurately. Then you are left to read 'to yourself'.

That is how the inner voice most of us have in our heads while we read becomes a habit. Instead of reading out loud we read silently. So when we talk about reading with your ears instead of your eyes – that is how it happens. You learn that you have to *hear* the words rather than see them to understand what you are reading.

**TIP** · · · · · · · · · · · · · · · · · · · · · · · · · · · · · · · · · · · · · · · · ·
*At the beginning of your education, reading 'to yourself' was slow because you were still learning to recognize the words fluently. As you read more and got further into the education system your reading rate increased because*

*your vocabulary increased. But your reading strategy didn't change.*

*As long as you are reading by saying each word to yourself in your mind, you will only ever be able to read as fast as you can speak – which for most people is between 150 and 250 words per minute.*

You can only hear or say one thing at a time but you can see millions of things at a time. Learning to speed-read is about learning to read with your eyes instead of your ears.

Reading is the slowest visual exercise we do. Look outside the nearest window for three seconds then close your eyes and say what you saw. How long did it take you to see what you saw and how long did it take you to say what you saw? Speaking to yourself when you read is the same as looking at a spectacular view or watching a film and, instead of visually understanding it, translating what you see into words that take several times longer to form, communicate and understand.

Visual and auditory memory are in different parts of the brain. When you first start to learn how to read with your eyes instead of your ears, your comprehension will diminish. This is perfectly normal. After a few hours of practice (in the beginning) and maybe 15 minutes a day for a few days you will find comprehension returning to what it was, and more long-term and integrated than you ever had it before. The same happens, for example, when you learn to touch type instead of looking at the keyboard and typing with one finger.

# Reading for comprehension

The aim of speed reading is to learn how to 'read' more than one word at a time. This leads to reading *phrases* rather than isolated words which goes a long way to helping you make sense of what you read. Meaning is in *groups* of words, so the more you are able to comprehend at one time the better your comprehension, understanding and subsequent recall will be. You understand more because you are reading in terms of ideas, thoughts and images rather than isolated words that mean nothing in themselves.

An exercise later today will help you increase your confidence in reading with your eyes instead of your ears.

# The biological challenge

Your eyes move very fast. They can process large amounts of information rapidly. If you read slowly, your eyes will tend to wander. The pacer will go a long way to help prevent that. Remember the exercise you did on Monday that showed you how differently your eyes moved when they had something to follow? Go back and refresh your memory if you need to.

Some eye movements you can do something about, some you can't.

## Fixation time

Your eyes need a certain amount of time to be able to absorb information. Try this experiment next time you are a passenger in a car. As the vehicle moves down the motorway, keep your eyes fixed on one point, not letting them settle on anything flying by the window. Does your view become blurred? Next, pick out certain parts of the landscape and follow them briefly. You might notice that what you look at becomes clear while the background is blurred. The same applies to reading. Your eyes need to rest – albeit it briefly – on groups of words, to be able to see them. The more words you can see and recognize in a single visual 'byte' the faster you will be able to read.

## Peripheral vision

Try an experiment: place your finger on the middle of the page and see as much as you can – where you are sitting, the room you are in, your surroundings. Your peripheral vision gives you the ability to see an enormous amount in a single visual byte. Now, without moving your eye from middle of the page, try to read the words on the edges of the page.

How did you do?

You will find that although you can see the words, you might not be able to 'read' them. When you were taught how to read you were taught to focus on one word at a time and not a whole line. Being able to expand what you can recognize within your peripheral vision takes practice. There are some exercises later in this section that will help you increase peripheral perception – you can do some of them while walking down the street.

## Regression and progression

These are visual tics. They are the result of poor concentration and lack of confidence in your memory.

*Regression* refers to the habit of going back to previous words or paragraphs to make sure you have understood them or remembered them accurately. *Progression* refers to the habit of jumping forwards for no particular reason.

Studies were done in the USA on how people's eyes moved when they read. Groups of people were given texts to read. At the bottom of the test piece was the figure $3,000,000.00. Every single person's eyes moved to the bottom of the text before they had read half the page to see what the $3,000,000.00

figure was all about. In terms of wasting time several things happen when you do this.

- You forget what you have just read.
- Your comprehension drops because you are reading something out of context.
- You lose time when you have to track back to find where you left off before the distraction.

Reading with a pacer and following the five-step system will help to reduce these reading habits. The following exercises will help you further.

## Increasing your span of recognition within your peripheral vision

### Exercise directions
In the pyramid of numbers and letters on the following pages, focus on the hash mark down the centre of the pyramid. The aim is to see how much you can read in your peripheral perception. Write down what you can see. Note: don't move your eyes from the centre column. You will be tempted to focus on the end of each row, but for the purpose of the exercise try to keep your eye on the centre hash. You might notice several things.

- You might not be able to see some of the letters and numbers on the longer lines. This is quite normal. Your optic nerve enters your eye at that point creating a 'blind spot'.
- If your eyes are of equal strength, you may find that you can see more to the right of centre than you can to the left. This is because we read from left to right and our eyes are conditioned to look in that direction for new text. If you were brought up reading Arabic or Hebrew, you might find that you will be able to see more to the left instead of the right of centre.

### Exercise 1
Place your pacer on the hash and move it down the hash marks in the centre of the pyramid. Keep your eye in the centre. Write down what you see on either side of the hash mark without moving your eyes away from the centre.

```
          S  #  p
        2 E  #  7 e
      d R 8  #  E 5 a
    D 2 5 l 5  #  n G 5 8 9
  6 B 2 9 o 6 3  #  R 8 3 4 2 N l
3 9 g 9 2 E 5 4 n  #  8 5 2 i 4 u S 7
```

### Exercise 2
Follow the instructions in exercise one. Keep your eye on the central column of letters and write down what you can see on either side.

| WG | H | PF |
|----|---|----|
| KD | T | OL |
| VS | K | DA |
| YO | E | NL |
| PZ | R | NJ |
| 5S | I | B9 |

### Exercise 3
Repeat the above instructions, with the following columns.

| only if    | armbands   | existed but  |
|------------|------------|--------------|
| once a     | bee        | swam in      |
| a three    | legged     | race he      |
| got half   | way        | to the other |
| end of the | beer glass | but was      |

Did you find the words any easier to read than the random letters? The words didn't make much sense either. Try this next exercise.

### Exercise 4
Beginning to read more than one word at a time: read the text as quickly as possible, keeping your eyes in the middle of the pyramid.

Winter
should be here by now
to seize the trees, our knees, the bees,
But every living breathing being
from bats to cats to sows to cows
Is basking in this balmy breeze
when normally man and beast should freeze.

Summer
might be looking down
So bright the sight with such delight,
And think her warming job is done
Courtesy of the winter sun,
So come mid year when nights should glow
We might be deep in cold white snow.

# Reading with your eyes instead of your ears

This next exercise will illustrate to you the difference between reading with your ears or your eyes. The more you practise it the better you will get at trusting what you see without having to hear it.

**Exercise 5**
Recognition exercise:

1 Cut a piece of fairly thick card about 2 cm square.
2 Cover the letters and 'flash' them as fast as you can, then make a note of what you see.
3 Try to keep the pace at which you reveal the numbers and letters to yourself constant.

| | | | |
|---|---|---|---|
| 143 | Emc2 | tdp | inki |
| l46 | Lsp5 | 3Pq | blt9 |
| Heg | wini | olp | wom8 |
| 37R | rQwg | 3owm | 286r |
| 63l | 6The | tap | unlw |
| 53L | Hare | cim | te4q |
| Jo4 | M23p | 536 | wim2 |
| ThR | Luck | 592 | 241y |
| 2h7 | 7play | per | tolp |
| Jon | u89Un | ith | 154r |
| 8Em | Pking | kin | tosi |
| Em2 | 43Jub | min | 90Pp |
| 492 | krimb | map | 76yz |
| hEp | HatrP | 43T | jipx |

- For the third and fourth columns, note down two sets of letters and numbers at the same time (i.e. only write what you see every other line).
- Which column was easiest to do?
- Did you find that sometimes you mistook an 'S' for a '5'?
- Did you find the double lines more challenging than the single lines?
- Most important – did you find that the letters that most resembled words were immediately recognisable and easy to recall?

When you read with your eyes you don't need to hear the whole word in your mind to know what it says. Your brain only needs a portion of the word to be able to make sense of it.

Develop your own eye exercises and practise them as often as you have time to. If you are going to choose one exercise to develop your visual reading for your 21-day programme (see Saturday) then exercise five should be it.

## Peripheral vision and awareness

As you walk, look straight ahead and try to 'see' as much as you can in your whole visual range. Try to see what is to the extreme left or right, top or bottom of your visual field.

As you go, articulate what you see. After you have done this for a while sit down and read, using your guide, as fast as you can and see the difference in the speed and ease of your reading. This is an excellent exercise to do while you are walking through town or a park.

# How to prevent and cure eyestrain

Your eyes need rest. The more relaxed they are, the longer you will be able to read. Here are a few simple things you should do to prevent and cure eyestrain.

1 Even before you feel tired, rest your eyes by closing them for a few moments every ten or 15 minutes.
2 As often as you remember to, palm. Palming is an excellent eye-relaxing exercise. Rub your hand together until they are warm, then close your eyes and cover them with your hands so that no light gets in. Do not press against your eyeballs: if

you were to do so, you could damage them. Cover your eyes like this for as long as you have the time.

3 Blink – The scratchy feeling in your eyes is probably there because they are dry. Many people who have eye problems compound them by not blinking and watering the eyes. While you are reading (especially from a PC monitor) be aware of your eyes and blink often. If it helps, put a sign above your PC reminding yourself to blink.

4 If your eyes feel particularly tired, there are a number of very good eye washes you can get from any pharmacy. Follow the instructions carefully when you use them. Check with your optician or your doctor.

5 If you wear contact lenses, it is even more important to take care of your eyes while you are reading. If you have a lot of reading to do, it might be advisable to take your lenses out. Carry a pair of glasses with you so that you can swap.

6 When you read, your eyes are limited in how much they can move. An excellent way to relieve stress is to practise some eye-robics. First, look straight ahead, then look up as far as you can, down as far as you can, to the left and to the right. Then, look to the top left, top right, bottom right and bottom left. Hold each gaze for only a second or so. When you have done that, squeeze your eyes shut and, if you want to, repeat the exercise. After you have completed the exercise, palm for a few minutes.

 **NEVER rub your eyes directly on the eyeball. There is nothing to protect the eye from damage when you do that.**

# Reading from a PC monitor without straining your eyes

There is much you can do to make reading from a monitor less stressful on your eyes. Here are a few tips.

● **Font size and type** – if someone has sent you a document and the font is difficult to read either due to its size or type, change it.

- **Screen contrast** – make sure the background contrasts the text on the screen. Sometimes a white screen might be too strong and a blue one too dark. A pale blue screen is quite a good one to read from.
- **Screen interference** – have as little around your screen as possible. Sometimes it is tempting to have all the icons on display. The more you have around your screen, the smaller the screen space is. Only have what is necessary for the work you are doing.
- **Screen savers** – there are screen savers on the market now that remain active all the time. The one that held my attention for quite some time was a sheep that ran around my screen while I worked. Not only does it help to relax your eyes and prevent you from staring at the screen, but a sheep chasing frogs across the screen is good for your sense of humour and anything good for your sense of humour is good for your stress levels, which in turn is good for concentration.
- **Screen position** – keep the screen a comfortable distance away from you. It should be at least an arm's length away. Also, avoid having the screen right in front of a window. The contrast in light can be uncomfortable and the activity outside can be distracting.
- **Comfort** – working at a PC means that the only part of your body that gets any exercise are your fingers. Stop, stretch your body and do the eye-robics every 20 to 30 minutes.

# Summary

A pacer will help you increase your reading rate by keeping your focus where it should be and your eyes moving across the page. Your aim is to gather the information you need without relying on the voice in your head or saying every word because, for as long as you hear each word in your head, you'll never be able to read any faster than you can speak.

When you start learning to speed-read you will probably find that the first thing that happens is the voice in your head starts talking really quickly. This is fine, but with practice you'll break the barrier and learn to understand what you're reading based on what you see rather than what you hear. At that point, the speed at which you read will increase rapidly.

This is not a technique you use while reading fiction or poetry or even when relaxing with the Sunday paper.

It's important to remember that applying speed-reading strategies to work-related material through the week won't affect your ability to enjoy a good novel in the evening and at weekends, a quality poem over coffee or the papers over breakfast. You can choose when to apply these techniques and when not to.

Give yourself time, be patient, but more important, be persistent. Use a pacer on all non-fiction you read, no matter where you find it. If people look at you strangely, it doesn't matter – you're the one increasing your reading rate.

SUNDAY

MONDAY

TUESDAY

WEDNESDAY

THURSDAY

FRIDAY

SATURDAY

# Questions

1. What are your most important tools for reading?
   a) A spade to bury the book ❏
   b) Your eyes ❏
   c) A match ❏
   d) A pillow ❏

2. What is the average speed at which people will read if they haven't learned how to speed-read?
   a) Less than 100 words per minute ❏
   b) Between 150 and 250 words per minute ❏
   c) Between 250 and 500 words per minute ❏
   d) Between 500 and 750 words per minute ❏

3. Why do we read one word at a time?
   a) That's how the brain works. ❏
   b) It's easy. ❏
   c) It's how we were taught. ❏
   d) It makes sense. ❏

4. For as long as you have the voice in your head, what's the fastest you'll be able to read?
   a) Between 250 and 500 words per minute ❏
   b) Between 500 and 750 words per minute ❏
   c) Between 750 and 1000 words per minute ❏
   d) As fast as you can speak ❏

5. Without training, what is the slowest work our eyes carry out?
   a) Star gazing ❏
   b) Watching a movie ❏
   c) People watching ❏
   d) Reading ❏

6. Fixation time refers to:
   a) length of time you're able to concentrate. ❏
   b) length of time it takes to fix something. ❏
   c) length of time your eyes need to focus on something before you see it clearly. ❏
   d) a small coastal town in Texas. ❏

7. On the subject of reading, 'regression' refers to:
   a) a visual tic that sends your eyes back to the start of the page. ❏
   b) something you do to remember your early childhood. ❏
   c) a visual tic that sends your eyes ahead looking for anything on the page that interests you. ❏
   d) something that happens when you get really angry. ❏

8. On the subject of reading, 'progression' refers to:
   a) a commune in California that attracts forward thinkers and visionaries. ❏
   b) a visual tic that sends your eyes ahead looking for anything on the page that interests you. ❏
   c) a visual tic that sends your eyes back to the start of the page. ❏
   d) thinking about something else rather than concentrating on what you're reading. ❏

9. The best way to prevent eyestrain is:
a) plenty of rest. ❏
b) plenty of good light. ❏
c) palming your eyes. ❏
d) blinking. ❏

10. What can you do to your PC to avoid eyestrain?
a) Increase the font size. ❏
b) Avoid clutter on your screen. ❏
c) Avoid dark backgrounds. ❏
d) All of the above. ❏

# THURSDAY

# Distractions and solutions

Although sore eyes leading to a headache can be one of the biggest distractions, there are any number of personal and environmental factors that will distract you from focusing on what you're trying to read. In an ideal world we would read only what interests us, in a perfect environment, with as much time as we needed, when we wanted. However, life isn't like that. We sometimes have to read material we aren't particularly interested in, at a time and place not suited to our reading style and, all to often, with a deadline looming.

External distractions like a ringing phone, too much noise in an open office or bright sun shining through your window can be switched off or blocked out relatively easily, but what happens inside your head is far more challenging to deal with. Thoughts about your weekend, upcoming holiday or dinner tonight won't stop you seeing the words on the page, but they'll guarantee you don't remember them. Add to that the idea that you might be reading a jargon-packed technical document that you've got little or no interest in and you might as well pack it in, put your feet up and plan the holiday you've got going in your imagination.

Or, you can learn to refocus your mind despite your distractions.

# Lack of concentration

If your attention drifts easily, inconsequential things distract you and you find it hard to concentrate, an easy solution may exist.

We discussed concentration and focus on Tuesday. If you think it might be helpful to go back to refresh your memory, try one of Tuesday's concentration exercises. The following tips will help increase your concentration and your ability to focus on one task.

● If you're reading a single document and need peak concentration to get through it, then take breaks often – approximately five minutes every 30 minutes. If you are reading a number of different texts and taking notes as you go, you can stretch your reading time to 45 minutes or an hour before you take a five or ten minute break. Pay attention to your body as you read. When you start yawning, making mistakes, re-reading passages or developing a headache it is time for a break. If you work through the symptoms of tiredness, your concentration, ability to remember and to understand what you are reading will diminish rapidly. Taking a break does not mean lying down and going to sleep for 20 minutes (although that does help) – go for a walk, drink some water, do something different.

- Know your *reasons for reading*. On Sunday and Monday, we discussed the importance of knowing why you are reading something. The clearer your purpose, the easier it will be to concentrate. As with many things in life – if you know what your reasons are for doing something, it is easier to do it, even when you don't really want to. If you have no reason, however, you are likely to give up fairly quickly.

- *Read actively* using a pacer, especially if you're feeling tired or if the material is challenging. The more senses you use, the more alert you're likely to remain. Imagine eating a meal and all you could do was see it. You couldn't smell it, taste it, feel the texture of the food or hear the sounds of cutting and slicing a juicy dish. All you could do was see it and eat it. How much do you think you would enjoy it? 80 per cent of the enjoyment is in the sensory appreciation of the meal: the taste, smell, texture and presentation of the food. The same applies to reading. Unfortunately, we are taught at a very early age to appreciate reading only through one sense. When you start building mind-maps, taking notes, thinking, discussing and actively reading, you will find that reading becomes more like the meal you can see, taste, smell, hear and feel. You almost always remember a good meal when the company is entertaining and the surroundings are pleasant. Treat reading like a good meal – you'll be surprised.

- Set a definite *time limit*. Break your reading into chunks. The chunks should be small enough to feel easily manageable and big enough to feel that you are achieving your goal. Be realistic. If, as you read, you find that the size of the chunks are too big or too small, stop and reassess. Be flexible.

# External distractions

Some people can concentrate because of the noise and chaos around them and some people can concentration in spite of it. If you're not one of them, do everything you can to minimize the noise around you.

- *Use earplugs* – if you get the right type they can be very comfortable and effective. Most good chemists will supply them. Try out a few makes and then keep a few sets on your desk.
- Wear headphones to *listen to appropriate music* – music without words and not too loud. Baroque music is best for maximum concentration; approximately 55–60 beats per minute. Make sure it's not too melancholy and only play music you enjoy. Experiment with music. Put one composer on for 20 minutes, change to another and then compare how you feel or how well you concentrate.
- If you work in a truly open-plan space – no dividers between the desks – *creating* a *visual barrier* between you and the people around you will help cut out distraction. You do not have to build a wall around you; this is not always desirable or possible. All you need do is place something on your desk that reaches eye level. This will provide a psychological barrier between you and the distracting environment, making it easier to cope with.
- If at all possible, leave the noisy environment and *find a quiet space* to read in. A delegate in one of my workshops would go into the cleaning closet when he had a very important document to read that needed all of his attention. He would go into the closet, jam the door shut, read the document, take the notes he needed and when he was finished he would come out. It worked for him and he was lucky enough to have a cleaning closet nearby with plenty of light and a bit of space, a supply of fresh air and no fumes.

# Internal distractions

Internal noise is caused by your mind wandering, perhaps because you have not fully and consciously committed to spend the time on a particular task. The guidelines on concentration will help you here. But what will help most is the decision to take the time to read.

If you don't make a firm decision to sit down and read, the type of internal talk that goes through your head might sound like this: 'I don't have the time for this ... X really needs to be done now ... Y will have to move to this afternoon ... I should be doing Z ...' There will be so much 'noise' in your head that you will be unlikely to remember one word you have read and will be wasting time.

● Make a decision to allocate a certain amount of time to read a set amount of material. If you can plan it into your day, do so. Some reading cannot be planned for. In this instance, instead of diving into the text without thinking, take time, go through the first two steps of the five-step system. Then, if you feel that the document does need to be read, decide when you are going to do it and put the time aside.
● When the decision is made, most internal talk will disappear and you will be able to focus.

# Physical distractions

## Tiredness

When you are tired you will find it almost impossible to concentrate. If you can take a break and go for a short nap or walk in the park, do so. If you can't do this, there are several other strategies open to you.

● Cut the time you spend reading down to ten- to 15-minute chunks.
● Use multi-sensory reading.
● Drink plenty of water
● Do aerobic exercises during your breaks – jump up and down a bit to get the oxygen flowing.

- Breathe deeply and stretch every few minutes.
- If you have music playing make it upbeat and energetic.
- Make sure you have a very good reason for reading through your tiredness.
- Do not go on more than you have to – stop when you are finished and take a good rest.
- Avoid working through the night.
- Avoid sugar.
- Avoid too much caffeine. For optimum performance you want to be alert not jittery.
- Reading at the right time of day can go a long way to preventing tiredness. You may notice that you can concentrate better at certain times of the day. Your results will be better if you read at those times.

# Sore eyes

Any kind of physical discomfort is a distraction. Your eyes are your primary tool for reading, so take care of them. For more details on eye care while reading, go back to Wednesday.

## Stress and reading

If you are stressed it is better to stop for a moment even if you feel you don't have the time. Stop, breathe, relax, evaluate the job, have a cup of tea or water and carry on. Being stressed does not make you read any faster or more effectively.

## Hunger and thirst

Hunger is a serious distraction. Similarly, if you eat too much, your concentration will be badly affected. If you have a large amount of reading to do, avoid eating too much at once and avoid excess sugar. Another cause of poor concentration is dehydration. Your body needs to be constantly replenished. When you feel thirsty, you are already dehydrated, so drink even if you don't feel you need to.

# Environmental issues

## Comfort

Ensure that you have fresh air and adequate light. Make yourself as comfortable as possible without feeling sleepy.

## Light

Daylight is best. If there is none, then there should not be too much contrast between the levels of light under which you are working and the rest of the room. This helps prevent eye strain. The main source of light should come over the shoulder opposite to your writing hand.

## Desk and chair

Make sure your desk and chair are the right height. When you are on your chair you should be able to sit back, with the chair supporting your back and your feet flat on the floor. If you cannot reach the floor place a block at your feet. Your desk should be large enough to take everything you need for the work you are doing.

# Work distractions

● **Plan your day.** Distractions come easily when you don't know what you want to achieve. At the start of your day write down everything you want to get done including what you want or need to read. Set aside a realistic amount of time. Add time for leisure reading! When you consciously put time in your day to read what you really want to read you will find that you enjoy the time, still get everything done and improve your speed reading by reading more.

● **Set ground rules.** When you start something, *finish it*. This will not only improve the quality of your work, it will increase the quantity of what you can achieve. You will also feel more relaxed and at ease because the job has been done and won't plague your mind as unfinished business.

# People demanding your attention

Few people have the luxury of being able to work without interruptions. There will always be someone, somewhere demanding your attention at some point, whether by phone, in person, by email, social media... the list goes on.

If you can, set aside the time you need to read and put up a 'do not disturb' notice.

If you are unable to do that, and most of us are, deal with interruptions like phone calls and people wanting to see you by consciously breaking off from your reading task and paying attention to the interruption.

If the phone rings or someone comes up to you while you are reading:

● finish the sentence or paragraph you are on, if at all possible
● place a mark on the place where you stopped
● briefly revise in your mind or on paper your understanding of the last sentence you read
● then, give attention to the next task.

Once the interruption is over, you can return to your reading, by:

● sitting for a moment to recall your understanding of the last sentence you read
● reaffirming your intention and purpose for reading
● setting the time again for a manageable chunk
● then, continuing to read.

Habit dictates that when we are interrupted we are very likely to 'hop' from one task to another. Taking a brief pause between tasks will ensure that you don't waste time trying to find where you left off. When you go back to your reading you will be able to begin immediately instead of having to sort out your ideas and remove confusion from your mind.

# Clearing your desk of distractions

- **Mail** – If you get a lot of mail at the beginning of the day have a routine of 20 minutes maximum each day to open it all and file it, deal with it or bin it. Don't let anything get in the way of doing that. It might not seem an important job at the time but when a week's mail piles up on your desk undealt with, it can be very distracting and waste more time than a short stress-free period set aside every day.
- **Desk space** – Every piece of paper on your desk will distract you several times every day. To minimize this type of distraction, make sure that the only things on your desk are those that have something to do with the project in hand. If you have your 'in' and 'out' trays on your desk, find another place for them for a week. At the end of the week, assess how differently you spent your time. When the tray is on your desk, all you have to do is look up and you will see everything else you have to do instead of being able to focus on one job at a time.

- **Clutter** – If your desk tends to be full of paper, clear it of *everything* other than the job at hand – for just one day – and see the difference. At the end of each day, make sure you leave your desk totally clear. In the morning you will feel far more relaxed and able to choose what you want to deal with instead of having to deal with whatever happens to be on the top of the pile.
- **Other people's reading** – Do not let anyone put anything on your desk that you haven't seen or agreed to have there, especially if you have to read it. When someone gives you something to read ask them to clearly explain why they think you have to read it and then decide if you want to accept it as an activity in your schedule. If they cannot give you an answer, think carefully before you accept it because once you have, you will be committed to doing it.

## Vocabulary

The better your vocabulary the faster you will be able to read. For more details see Monday's section on speed reading.

# Summary

The number of distractions around you – internal or external – is infinite: aches and pains, itchy feet, tired eyes, stress through the day, tight deadlines, an over-demanding boss, memories of your last holiday, plans for your next holiday, ideas for the weekend, too much noise around you, too little noise around you, ringing in your ears ...

You could deal with the distraction by eliminating it – but this might create a new problem because eliminating it might mean booking the holiday you're thinking about, calling the friend you can't get out your head or dropping down to the local coffee shop for a brew and turning what was a mere distraction into procrastination.

The real solution is (I might have said this before!) to have a clear purpose, which could be anything from finding the answer to a specific question to wanting to have a general understanding of the subject in 20 minutes. By applying the five-step system you will not only get through your reading in record time, you will also be able to remember what you read and apply it when you need to.

If you find you are still distracted despite applying the five-steps then put your reading away, go and do something else and come back to it later.

SUNDAY
MONDAY
TUESDAY
WEDNESDAY
THURSDAY
FRIDAY
SATURDAY

# Questions

1.  What are the most difficult
    distractions to deal with when
    we read?
    a)  Other people ❏
    b)  Outside demands ❏
    c)  Deadlines ❏
    d)  What goes on inside our own
        head ❏

2.  What can you do to ensure peak
    concentration?
    a)  Take breaks often ❏
    b)  Have a reason to read ❏
    c)  Read actively ❏
    d)  Set a time limit ❏

3.  What are the best ways to
    minimize external distractions?
    a)  Wear earplugs. ❏
    b)  Create barriers around you
        if you're in an open plan
        environment. ❏
    c)  Do difficult work away
        from the office. ❏
    d)  Listen to your type
        of music. ❏

4.  When your mind keeps drifting
    while you read, what are your
    options?
    a)  Take a break. ❏
    b)  Focus on what you're
        reading, get it done, then
        move on to whatever is
        drifting through your head. ❏
    c)  Deal with the distraction and
        get back to work. ❏
    d)  All of the above,
        depending on what's
        drifting through your mind
        and how important it is. ❏

5.  What do physical distractions
    include?
    a)  Sore eyes ❏
    b)  Tiredness ❏
    c)  Stress ❏
    d)  Aches or pains ❏

6.  What can you do to ensure your
    work environment is designed
    for maximum concentration?
    a)  Cover the floor with
        beanbags. ❏
    b)  Pipe whale sounds into the
        office. ❏
    c)  Make sure your desk
        and chair height are
        comfortable and adjust
        the lighting to suit. ❏
    d)  Wear a kaftan into the
        office and soak your feet
        in bath salts. ❏

7.  What are the most effective ways
    to avoid distractions at work?
    a)  Plan your day. ❏
    b)  Set ground rules. ❏
    c)  When you start something,
        finish it. ❏
    d)  All of the above. ❏

8.  How can you avoid distractions
    from people while you read?
    a)  Finish the sentence or
        paragraph before you
        engage with the person
        speaking to you. ❏
    b)  Place a mark where you
        left off. ❏
    c)  Take a second to run
        mentally through
        what you just read. ❏
    d)  Pay attention to the person
        demanding it, when you're
        ready. ❏

9. How can you clear your desk of distractions?
a) Clear your mail every day. ❑
b) Clear the clutter off your desk. ❑
c) Make sure everything on your desk has a reason to be there. ❑
d) Don't let anyone else's reading become your priority (unless it's your job). ❑

10. Does what you eat through the day impact your ability to concentrate?
a) No, I can eat anything and I have tons of energy through the day. ❑
b) A heavy lunch knocks me out for the afternoon. ❑
c) I need sugar to keep me going. ❑
d) I don't know... I'll take a week to carefully consider what I eat to see how it affects my moods, energy levels and concentration. ❑

# FRIDAY

# Reading different types of material for different reasons

Most people will learn one reading strategy when they're at school – left to right, beginning to end, one word at a time – and apply that to everything they read from newspapers to novels to technical documents ...for the rest of their lives.

However, if you follow the five-step system you'll soon realize that your reasons for reading a newspaper or novel or technical document are different and, as a result, the strategy you apply to each should also be different.

You might want to apply the full five-step system to a work-related document, but you certainly won't want to apply it to a novel. Likewise, you'll read a Sunday paper differently based on whether it's over breakfast or is part of your PR job.

Now that you've learned the five-step system, you can bend it and reshape it to suit any type of reading material, no matter what your reasons for reading it.

The same applies to the memory techniques you use. If you're reading something for general interest you'll use a different memory technique from when you read material you might be examined on.

The challenge you face as you learn to apply the five-step system is falling into the bad habit of using one technique for everything. Be flexible, use different strategies and you'll find you'll want to read more because the time you spend reading effectively will be time well spent.

# Reading different types of material

The way you approach a document (book, newspaper, memo, email etc.) should be driven by your purpose.

## Technical material

This type of reading can be fairly easy because most technical writing is well structured. Also, it will be rare that you have to read and remember everything about the text without being able to refer to it later on when you need to. For this type of reading apply the five-step system in its entirety and use a memory system that works well for you. Use mind-maps. If you don't like mind-maps, try a process map. This technique, similar to a flow chart, allows you to see how information, ideas and practices are linked and what effect they have on each other.

## Non-fiction for leisure

This is probably the easiest of all reading simply because you are interested in the subject. Most non-fiction, like technical writing, is also fairly well structured so the five-step process can be readily applied.

It is easy to become absorbed in 'work'-related reading and not put time aside for leisure reading and knowledge gathering. Once you are comfortable with speed reading and the five-step process, you will find that non-fiction is the ideal material to practise on. Enjoy taking the time for this type of reading. If you have 'work' to do, you might feel uncomfortable or guilty about taking time out for leisure, albeit non-fiction, reading. A good way to get around this is to make part of your purpose increasing your reading skill so that you will be able to read 'work' material more effectively. Besides, if you only ever read text that bores you, your passion for reading will soon be subdued. Make the time to read what you want to read.

# Reading for study

More and more people are studying as well as coping with a full-time job. Here is a way to structure your reading so that you succeed without causing yourself undue stress and giving up on life for a few years.

- Determine how many study days you have before the exam or end of the course. Be realistic about this. If you are working full time as well as studying, then remember that you will only have mornings, evenings and weekends and that you also have to fit a life in somewhere.
- Establish exactly how much material you have to get through to complete the course or module. Generally you will have a number of books, perhaps a few CDs or DVDs, a few television or online programmes, and some notes from lectures. Gather all the material together into one place so that you can see that the amount of information you have to learn is finite. This does the soul good.
- Go through the course notes and make a list of all the different sub-topics you have to cover. This allows you to break the overall subject into manageable chunks.
- Under each sub-topic write down the chapters, CDs, DVDs and lectures (all sources) you have to refer to for information.
- Organize the sub-topics into an 'information order'. Some will serve as good background for others so cover those first. The order you study each sub-topic in is entirely up to you and dependent on your current knowledge base.
- Once all sub-topics are identified and sources are gathered you will be able to create a realistic and achievable timetable.
- The timetable you create should not have you waking up at 4 a.m. and going to sleep at midnight. You will burn out. Make space in your timetable for Quality Recover Time (QRT). Have plenty of it.
- Create a good study space. This space should only be used for study if possible.
- Enjoy the learning process by rewarding yourself for each accomplishment (at least once a day).

# Reading for research

The good thing about reading for research is that your purpose is very clearly defined and you are looking for something quite specific. Apply the five-step system and follow the guidelines for 'reading for study'.

# Reading for work (especially mail, emails and memos)

The rule here is 'be selective'. The trouble with reading that you do for work is that there will probably be a resulting activity for each document. Before you read anything, especially if it is likely to take you a while or if it seems to land on your desk often, ask a few questions first:

● Who wants you to read it?
● Why do they want you to read it?
● What do you have to do with the information once you have read it?

Once you have ascertained that there are good reasons for you reading the documents, take the following steps:

● Decide how much time you are going to spend reading incoming mail, emails, articles or reports.
● Scan the documents for structure and key ideas with one thing in mind – can any of them go in the bin? Then sort them into two piles – one of which goes straight into the bin, the other which requires further attention.
● Skim all of the documents that need further attention and ask one question of each – can this be filed or does it require action? Put the pile for filing aside to file.
● Actively read the remaining pile and, using post-it notes or writing directly on the letter or document, write what actions need to be taken.
● Finally, plan the actions into your day or week and file the documents so that you can retrieve them easily when you need them.

*Remember the clear-desk policy – only have papers on your desk for the job you are currently working on.*

## Newspapers

NOTE – this does not necessarily apply to the casual, relaxed Sunday morning reading of the paper, unless you want it to. Reading a newspaper should be approached with as much consideration as reading anything else. The five-step system works very well for papers, but it is not necessary to go through the entire five-step process in order. You can read a paper very quickly by following three very simple steps.

- State your purpose – are you reading to get an overview of the whole paper or are you looking for a particular story?
- Glance through the paper looking for key articles you're interested in. Read the headlines and first paragraphs. Go through the entire paper, circling the articles you would like to return to.
- Finally, speed read selected articles for the information you want.

*REMEMBER – these are only suggested guidelines. If you find another way of reading a paper even faster, then use whatever works for you.*

## Magazines

Reading a magazine (particularly a special interest or trade magazine) is slightly different to reading a newspaper. A newspaper is one of many sources of news. If you miss anything from the paper, you could get the story from the television, radio or Internet. Most magazines only come out once a month or once a quarter. A magazine should thus be treated like a small textbook. Follow all the steps of the five-step reading system to get the best out of a magazine. If there is information you are likely to need again there are several things you can do to make it easily accessible.

- Read the magazine with post-it notes to hand. As you find articles you are interested in, note the page number, title and brief summary (just a sentence or two) on the post-it note. Stick the post-it on the front page of the magazine and file it in a file dedicated to 'interesting articles'.
- If you don't want to keep the whole magazine then tear out the pages or photocopy the articles you want and file those away with a brief summary of what the article is about and what you might use it for later.

## Emails

Emails are a blessing or a curse depending on who is sending them. Rule one with emails is to do to others, as you want them to do to you. If you don't want a huge amount of junk in your in-box – don't send it! If you have someone who keeps sending you emails you don't want, whether it's jokes or stories, be firm and ask them not to. Like traditional mail, if you can see it is junk before you open the envelope – bin it.

A good way of viewing email is to have the feature on your system where your inbox screen is split. One half has a list of all the messages, and the other half lets you read the email without actually opening it. This saves time.

If there are attachments to the email and you need to read them fast then it might be better to print them out or use a piece of software like Spreeder.com. If you prefer to read from the screen there are some ideas on Wednesday on how to do that without straining your eyes.

## Novels

The more you read the faster you will become. Reading novels is excellent practice for speed-reading skills. Your reading rate will automatically increase when you are aware of your reading strategy and practise the reading system on non-fiction.

# Making the most of your available time

The most important thing about reading (for work or study, this does not apply to leisure reading unless you want it to) is planning. Here are some simple guidelines on how to make the most of your time.

- Read when you are feeling alert and refreshed. If you have to read and you are tired, drink plenty of water and take regular breaks.
- Plan what you have to read and set aside a little more time than you think you will need.
- When someone puts something on your desk expecting you to read it, find out whether it is really necessary. Perhaps someone can summarize it for you, rather than reading the whole document yourself.
- Make the bin the first option when you are sorting mail (including email).
- When you are going through your mail decide what you have to read and put non-urgent documents aside. If you have time at the end of the day to read them, then do so.

# How to get the message in the minutes before a meeting

'I only have five minutes and I have to sound like I know what I'm talking about.' Have you ever been in the situation where someone gives you a document and tells you that you are expected at a meeting in five minutes to discuss it with others who have probably had a day to read it?

Do you find that your mind goes blank and for some reason words and letters don't make sense anymore? This has more to do with stress and a lack of strategy than it does with time. When this happens, ask the document-giver:

● what it has to do with you – ask for background information.
● why you only have five minutes – this gives purpose and focus.
● to briefly summarize the text for you – this gives you content.

Once you have done that, complete steps 1 to 4 of the five-step system:

● State your purpose – why do you have to read this? What are you going to do with the information?
● Flick through the text reading any summaries and conclusions.
● Read through it again, this time looking for key words, significant figures or words in bold or italics.
● Read the first and last paragraphs of each section.
● Finally, if there is time, fill in the gaps by reading as much as you can, beginning with the first sentence of each paragraph and any bullet points (see step 4 of the five-step system).

*It is very important to remember, as you go through steps 1 to 4, to take notes, preferably on the document itself. The thoughts you have as you read will probably be what you would want to contribute to the meeting. If you don't write them down you might forget and lose valuable insights.*

## Going into the meeting

Before you go into the meeting, stop at the door, stand up straight, breathe in deeply and smile (relax). Once inside:

- Don't profess to be the expert on the subject.
- Listen first to what others have to say.
- Ask questions before you make statements.

You could bluff if others know less than you do but eventually you will be caught out. It's easier to find a reading strategy that gives you a chance of absorbing as much information as possible rather than struggling to look as if you know what you are talking about.

Once you take control you will relax and be able to concentrate successfully on the task.

# Finding the right information fast

When you have to find information fast, use steps 1, 2 and 3 of the five-step system.

- Be very clear about what you are looking for.
- Write your purpose down.

- Begin step 2 (structure) by highlighting any chapters or sections that look like they could contain the answers to your question. Use post-it notes to mark the relevant pages with a comment on them as to what you expect to find there.
- Once completed, begin step 3 by restating and reclarifying your purpose. What exactly are you looking for and what are the key words that would alert you to the answer?
- Skim or scan the pieces of text you identified during step two, looking for language and key ideas.

Stop as soon as you find your answer, unless you decide to continue.

When you read a document for the first time, read it with the intention of going back to it to find information at a later date. Mark relevant pages or take referencing notes. Writing a brief summary of each section in the margins is an excellent way to help you access information later. It is also a very good technique for remembering what you have read.

# The real world – reading under pressure

Sometimes there is not enough time to read what you have to. When this happens (and for some people it could be happening every day) you have to be disciplined about what you read and develop excellent prioritization skills.

A deadline can be one of the biggest distractions. Becoming wound up and stressed only defeats the object. When you have such a situation:

- Make a realistic assessment of the available time.
- Decide what you have to know.
- Decide what the best and fastest source of information is.
- If it is something you have to read, complete steps 1 to 3 of the five-step system and be very clear about cutting out what is not essential.
- Speak to someone who already knows something on the subject and gather as much information as possible.

- Find out exactly why you have such a tight deadline and find out whether it can be changed.
- After your questions have been answered, divide your reading into the amount of time you have, and focus, relax, breathe deeply, make sure you have a good supply of water.
- Take plenty of breaks. When you are under pressure it is more important to sit back and take stock than when you have all the time in the world. If you are under pressure and not taking care of yourself, stress will counteract all the work you are doing.

To avoid this happening repeatedly, it is important to be able to prioritize your reading and other tasks all the time, not just in an emergency.

# Summary

You'll now be able to apply the five-step system to every type of reading material and under any conditions, regardless of the tenacity of the distractions around you.

Have some fun with this and put yourself to the test. Take your reading into busy, noisy, difficult places, decide what you want to get out of it, set an amount of time and get through it regardless of what goes on around you.

Ultimately you want to be able to read any technical document in any high-stress environment, even if people are literally waiting in front of you for your response.

Your success will be a culmination of having a clear purpose (have I mentioned that before?), using the five-step system and having command of your mind and your emotions to ensure stress doesn't get in the way and slow you down.

No matter how much pressure you're under or how much you have to read, take the time to plan your reading and prioritize what's important. In the long run, it'll be the shortest route.

SUNDAY
MONDAY
TUESDAY
WEDNESDAY
THURSDAY
FRIDAY
SATURDAY

# Questions

1. You should use different reading strategies on different types of reading material.
   a) True ❑
   b) False ❑

2. Reading for pleasure will not be ruined when you learn to speed-read.
   a) True ❑
   b) False ❑

3. What time of the day is best for reading difficult, technical material?
   a) Early morning ❑
   b) Late afternoon ❑
   c) When the office is empty ❑
   d) When you feel most energized and alert, no matter what time of day it is or what's going on around you. ❑

4. What should be your first option when you're sorting mail (snail or e-mail)?
   a) Read everything to make sure it's not important. ❑
   b) File everything for later. ❑
   c) Bin it. ❑
   d) Pass it on to someone else to read. ❑

5. When you have only a few minutes to get to a meeting and you have to read something before you go in, you should:
   a) hide in the restroom. ❑
   b) panic. ❑
   c) leave the office for the day. ❑
   d) apply the five-step system. ❑

6. If you're at a meeting and you've only just familiarized yourself with a new document, you should:
   a) start talking and not stop until someone kicks you out. ❑
   b) hope no one has read it and wing it. ❑
   c) keep quiet and listen. ❑
   d) act mysterious if someone asks your opinion and pretend to know everything. ❑

7. When you need to find information fast, you should:
   a) get someone else to do it. ❑
   b) use the five-step system. ❑
   c) make it up and hope no one notices. ❑
   d) panic. ❑

8. When prioritizing your reading, you need to consider:
   a) what's important to you and your outcomes. ❑
   b) what you can do in the amount of time you have. ❑
   c) when and for what you need the information. ❑
   d) All of the above. ❑

9. If you need answers to questions and don't have a lot of time to get them, you should:
   a) use the five-step system on every form of written material you can get your hands on (paper and electronic). ❑
   b) speak to experts. ❑
   c) use every source. ❑
   d) All of the above. ❑

10. The key to successful speed reading is reading everything in detail.
    a) True ❑
    b) False ❑

# SATURDAY

## What next?

Whenever you learn something new there is a period when you know how to do it but haven't quite got it right yet. This is a most fragile time in learning. Receiving the information is easy – you read a book, go on a course, listen to a recording. Once the information is in your head, it's up to you whether you use the information or not. Do you put your course books on the shelf until 'later'? Do you put the book back on the bookshelf and think, 'Hmmm, interesting', and fall back into your old habits? What you do with your new information is entirely up to you. You can forget about it, or you can integrate what you have learned into the way you live, work and study.

It takes decision and action. The decision takes a split second. Are you going to become the best you can be?

After you make the decision it is important to build a plan.

Sometimes, when we are about to start something new, we believe that it is the only way to go and everything else in our lives must change to suit the new way. The problem is that when you try to change old habits, they fight back. One way of making the change process easy is to create a daily plan. Instead of doing everything in one day and being overwhelmed, complete the task a bit at a time.

# Guidelines for a 21-day programme

The first time I created one of these programmes I put aside four hours a day to the new task. The day started at 5 am and at 9 am I would have breakfast, go for a run and get on with the day. I lasted two days. I started too early, spent too long at it, crammed too much into the time and spent the rest of the day half asleep and irritable.

Rules for the 21-day programme are based on general commonsense.

- **Make your programme not too easy, not too difficult.** The programme you create must be easy enough for you to know it is achievable and challenging enough to excite you.
- **Select topics that interest you.** The material you read to develop your speed-reading skills should be interesting to you. During your normal working day you may come across plenty that you have to read that isn't too interesting.

- **Have variety.** On one day, practise speed reading with a novel, the next day, try a newspaper, after that practise with magazines you have wanted to read for a while. Each time the aim is to read as much as you can, using the most effective technique possible.
- **Put aside 20 minutes each day to practise speed-reading exercises (see Monday).** Twenty minutes is a guideline. If you only have ten minutes then that would do fine, as long as every day you are spending some focused time working on your new skill. The best time to do this is in the morning because it will remind you to pay attention to your reading as the day goes by. If you can only put 20 minutes aside in the evening then remind yourself in the morning when you plan your day that you have put that time aside and that you will be aware of your reading throughout the day.
- **Integrate your new knowledge into what you already do during the day.** Use your new skill every time you read something: your mail, letters, newspapers, books, emails, memos, the backs of cereal boxes – anything.
- **Keep your purpose clear.** If you do not have a purpose you will quickly lose interest. Keep in mind why you are learning how to read fast. What else do you want to do with the extra time you have? What will speed reading give you?

- **Practise daily.** The more consistent your practice is the better you will become. If you speed-read on one day and forget for the next few, the chances are that the number of days between practices will just increase.
- **Teach someone else.** When you can teach someone else what you have learned, you have learned it well. If you have children, teach them – any time is a good time for them to learn. If you can't answer all their questions use the five-step process to find the answers.
- **Read in groups.** Developing a reading group is an excellent way to ensure you practise. Meet once a month or more often if you like. Make the purpose of the group twofold; firstly, discuss the contents of the book, articles or papers you read, and second, discuss the reading methods you used or had trouble with. Also, begin to explore other ways of reading effectively and bring that to the group. This way, group motivation will drive your learning forward. The more people you involve in your learning the easier it will be to stay motivated. It helps if there is someone there to help you along when you are having difficulties.
- **Learn something new every day.** No matter how small, learn something new. Keep a notebook for your mini lesson of the day and you will be surprised how fast your general knowledge grows.
- **Learn a new word every day.** The better your vocabulary is the faster you will be able to read.
- **Be flexible.** If you find that your programme is too easy or too difficult, change it.
- **Don't stop after 21 days.** After your first 21 days you will have integrated the basics of speed reading successfully. After that, take your reading to another level. You have already developed the habit of putting aside time to practise a new skill: keep that time available. Keep reading.

Opposite is a table you can use as a template to design your 21-day programme.

| Day | Reading material / purpose | Time | What did I learn? | New word |
|---|---|---|---|---|
| 1 | The morning paper in 20 minutes or less. To practise five steps and gain information. | 20 min (0600–0620) | [In this column write the most interesting thing you learned.] | [At least one new word and its definition.] |
| 2 | | | | |
| 3 | | | | |
| 4 | | | | |
| 5 | | | | |
| 6 | | | | |
| 7 | | | | |
| 8 | | | | |
| 9 | | | | |
| 10 | | | | |
| 11 | | | | |
| 12 | | | | |
| 13 | | | | |
| 14 | | | | |
| 15 | | | | |
| 16 | | | | |
| 17 | | | | |
| 18 | | | | |
| 19 | | | | |
| 20 | | | | |
| 21 | | | | |

Another useful tool is to keep a small notebook (together with your 21-day programme) to write down comments on the day's reading activities. What did you feel or think as you read? What was easy? What was difficult? What would you change about the way you read that day? What questions do you have?

# A to Z of effective reading

**A**  **Active reading** – Take notes, write in margins, circle, highlight, underline, think, argue, debate your way through whatever you read.

**B**  **Believe** – You are capable of phenomenal things. Make this only your first step to effective reading. Look constantly for a better way of doing what you do.

**C**  **Concentration** – Practise concentration techniques; remember that without concentration there is no memory, whether you are reading or remembering names.

**D**  **Determination** – Frustration is a natural part of the learning process. Learn to enjoy it.

**E**  **Enjoy** – The more you enjoy reading the less stressed you will be and the better you will remember what you read.

**F** **Flexibility** – Remember that you don't have to read fast all the time. Develop the skill of being able to identify when you can read fast and when you have to slow down.

**G** **Groups** – Sometimes a group of brains is better at staying motivated than one working alone.

**H** **Harassed** – If you are feeling stressed or tired your effectiveness will diminish. Stop and take a break especially if you feel you do not have the time.

**I** **Ideas** – Cross-reference, combine and elaborate on ideas between texts.

**J** **Justify** – Always ask yourself why you have to read it and what call it will have on your time.

**K** **Knowledge** – Make increasing your knowledge of yourself and the world around you a daily goal.

**L** **Learn** – Make it a habit to learn something new from your reading every day.

**M** **Manageable chunks** – Avoid reading for more than 30 minutes at a time.

**N** **Novels** – Using the five-step system for novels could spoil the ending. You will find, however, that the speed at which you can read novels will increase as a result of your speed-reading practice. You will not lose any of the enjoyment, in fact, you might find you finish more of the novels that you begin.

**O** **Organized** – Clear your desk of everything other than what you are working on at the time.

**P** **Purpose** – Have a clear and definite purpose whenever you read anything.

**Q** **Question** – Always ask questions. Just because what the author has said is in print, does not mean that he or she is right.

**R** **Revise** – Refer to notes you have made previously whenever you have the opportunity to do so. Sometimes what we think at the time we only appreciate later.

**S** **Stretch** – Your body is involved in your reading as well as your mind. Reading is physically passive. When you read for any length of time your body will become stiff and sore. Stretch whenever you take a break.

**T   Time** – Take time to develop any new skill. Enjoy the gap between knowing you don't know how to do something and achieving success. Be patient with yourself.

**U   Use** – The more you use the information you learn the better you will remember it and will be able to apply it when you need it.

**V   Vocabulary** – Use steps 2 and 3 (structure and language) to identify words you don't understand. Look them up before you continue. If you encounter a word you don't understand while you are reading, take note, keep going and look it up at the end of the paragraph or section. You might find that the meaning becomes clear in the context of the text.

**W   Work is play with a suit on** – Make whatever you do fun and you will be able to carry on longer and perform more effectively.

**X   X-plore** – Find information from as many different sources as possible. Sometimes what you are looking for in a text you can get more quickly from a phone call to an expert or a friend.

**Y   You** – Reading and learning is a personal skill. Make sure that the techniques you use work for you. Try a variety of different ways of reading and learning and create a set of tools that suits you.

**Z   ZZZ Sleep** – Avoid reading and studying at the expense of a good night's sleep. Take breaks whenever you need them. Read something enlightening, but light, before you go to sleep and think of what it means to you.

For more information on this series, this book, the author and further books by Hodder & Stoughton, visit www.inaweek.co.uk and www.tinakonstant.com

# Summary

You should by now:

- have learned, applied and practised the five-step system
- have increased your reading rate by learning to read based on what you see rather than what you hear
- have started to use a variety of memory techniques based on what you're reading and when you'll need to use the information
- be treating your eyes with more respect
- be learning to adjust how you read based on the material and your environment
- be integrating what you have learned in this book into how you think and work and read until this new habit replaces the old, and effective reading becomes 'how you do things'.

Do yourself a favour and have one last big sort through old magazines, documents, manuals and newspapers that you have allowed to build up, and then throw your in-tray away.

Don't let unread material build up. There's no need. You now have the skills to get through the reading that lands on your desk as it comes in. If you really want to read it later, spend a couple of minutes doing steps 1 to 4 on the material, put a note on the cover outlining why you're keeping it and how it might be useful later, then put it away with the intention of picking it up and doing step 5 when you actually need it.

Take control of your time, your knowledge and how you action it. In doing so you'll be taking control of your life.

# Questions

1. The best way to fully integrate the new skills in this book is to use them in your everyday reading.
   a) True ❏
   b) False ❏

2. Your 21-day programme should include:
   a) topics that interest you ❏
   b) daily practice ❏
   c) reading in groups ❏
   d) all of the above. ❏

3. Your 21-day programme should:
   a) be not too easy and not too difficult. ❏
   b) integrate new knowledge with what you already know. ❏
   c) include about 20 minutes to simply practise speed reading (step 5). ❏
   d) have plenty of variety. ❏

4. You should learn a new word every day so that you can:
   a) mess with your friends. ❏
   b) increase your reading rate. ❏
   c) improve your general knowledge and understanding of language. ❏
   d) All of the above. ❏

5. It's important to create a work environment you like to be in.
   a) True ❏
   b) False ❏

6. There is a known limit to the speed at which you can read.
   a) True ❏
   b) False ❏

7. The key to the five-step reading system is:
   a) having a purpose (even if it changes). ❏
   b) applying it to everything, no matter how long or short, fact or fiction. ❏
   c) using it when you remember to. ❏
   d) using it only for work. ❏

8. You should be flexible in your reading – read to suit the material, what you want from it and your environment.
   a) True ❏
   b) False ❏

9. You have to practise steps 1 to 4 of the five-step process or you'll never get it right.
   a) True ❏
   b) False ❏

10. It's important to take breaks while you read because:
    a) it helps maintain concentration. ❏
    b) it relaxes you, and the less stressed you are, the easier it'll be to concentrate. ❏
    c) it allows you to think about what you read. ❏
    d) walking around and stretching your body is as important as taking care of your eyes. ❏

# 7 × 7

## 1 Seven key ideas

- Always have a purpose. Know why you're reading something – even if it's just because you want to.
- Use the five-step system to identify what you want to focus on and eliminate what you don't need. Don't fall into the trap of thinking you need to know everything all the time – you'll never keep up.
- Know what you will be using the information for before deciding which reading or memory technique to apply.
- Share the load. If you can, split the required reading between a few people then get together and share the knowledge.
- When reading technical material keep a list of acronyms, key terms and definitions handy. It will save a huge amount of time as you read.
- Read a book a week by dividing the number of pages of a book by seven and reading those pages each day. You'll be surprised how quickly you can get through 50 or so pages a day. By the end of the year you'll have read 52 books!
- Challenge yourself. Read books you'd usually avoid.

## 2 Seven best recourses

- Software to help you read digital content faster: http://ereflect.com/
- Stretch your mind. Try photoreading: http://www.photoreading.com/
- Tony Buzan is great for information on mind-maps, memory techniques and speed-reading in general: http://www.tonybuzan.com/
- Get to grips with time and how you manage it. Brian Tracy's *Eat That Frog* (Berrett-Koehler, 2007) is a good start.
- Join a local book club or, if you don't have one, join the Goodreads book club (www.goodreads.com). It's a great collection of people who read a huge variety of books. You can of course, start your own book club.
- Subscribe to a 'book summaries' site. Do a search for those key words and choose one that suits your needs. These are sites where you can find summaries of some very amazing books.
- If you have any questions visit www.tinakonstant.com and get in touch through email, twitter or Facebook.

# 3 Seven great quotes

- 'Knowledge Management is expensive – but so is stupidity!' Thomas Davenport
- 'The more that you read, the more things you will know, the more that you'll learn, the more places you'll go.' Dr. Seuss
- 'Learn from yesterday, live for today, hope for tomorrow. The important thing is not to stop questioning.' Albert Einstein
- 'If you only read the books that everyone else is reading, you can only think what everyone else is thinking.' Haruki Murakami
- 'To read without reflecting is like eating without digesting.' Edmund Burke
- 'There is more treasure in books than in all the pirate's treasure on Treasure island.' Walt Disney
- 'It is what you read when you don't have to that determines what you will be when you can't help it.' Oscar Wilde

# 4 Seven things to avoid

- Avoid reading work/research material from beginning to end.
- Avoid reading what you don't want or need to read. If a book doesn't meet your needs, ditch it! You don't have to finish a book just because you started it. Your time is too valuable.
- Avoid overload. Prioritize and deal with information as it comes in.
- Avoid taking on information you don't need just because someone says you must.
- Avoid buying into the idea that information from a specific source is a 'cure all'. Get what you need from all angles and perspectives. It will give you greater depth and detail.
- Avoid forgetting what you read by having a purpose, applying an appropriate memory technique and applying the knowledge you gather.
- Avoid falling back into old habits by using every opportunity to read faster and more efficiently.

# 5 Seven inspiring people

- Sir Richard Branson grew up with dyslexia yet gathered the knowledge and information he needed to build an empire.
- Nelson Mandela: 'Education is the most powerful weapon which you can use to change the world.' Need I say more? Here is a man who never ceased to learn and grow despite undeniable hardships.
- Howard Berg is in the 1990 *Guinness Book of World Records* for reading 25,000 words a minute.
- Einstein was spectacular at turning accepted beliefs on their heads. His take on reading (too much): 'Any man who reads too much and uses his own brain too little falls into lazy habits of thinking'. Read all you like, but if you don't think...
- Malala Yousafzai – shot for wanting to go to school, then standing up to an entire culture for her rights and the rights of others to be educated.
- Robert E. Kahn and Vint Cerf – 'the fathers of the Internet' which in turn led to the technology we have today to create and share more knowledge (and nonsense) than ever before.
- The person who read to you as a child.

# 6 Seven things to do today

- Use the five-step system on a non-fiction book you've been avoiding.
- Practise speed-reading using a guide.
- Enhance your digital reading by trying out speed-reading software.
- Commit to using the information you read.
- Clear your desk. Just do it. Get the clutter out of your workspace once and for all.
- Choose a book you really want to read (fiction or non-fiction) and read at least 50 pages – then do the same tomorrow and the next day.
- Get through your reading as quickly as possible, then go play on the beach... in a park... up a mountain... in your garden...

# 7 Seven trends for tomorrow

- With the surge in self-publishing, mass opinion and information is only going to get bigger. It will get more difficult to identify qualified information from amateur contributions. Research the author for credibility before taking what they say as gospel.
- Reading is only one way to gather information. Make use of audio books, speedreading software and other technology.
- Teach your kids to manage information and read effectively. The better they handle information in the future, the better they'll do.
- Get practical. With so much information coming at us at such a pace, it's easy to get stuck in our heads and forget to use our hands. Pick up a practical hobby.
- As we become more independent of each other at work (working from home or on the road) the flow of information and knowledge will become more critical. Do your colleagues a favour and share what you have in a way they can easily understand.
- With so much amateur information spilling out through the internet, do the world a service and make sure what you contribute has great value.
- The speed of the world is increasing. There will be conflicting movements to slow things down. People will be looking for the simpler things in life which includes reading a good book by an open fire as the sun sets over the hills. Get in there early. Don't let the information age drag you under its wheels.

# Answers

**Sunday:** 1d; 2d; 3d; 4a; 5b; 6d; 7c; 8c; 9d; 10d;

**Monday:** 1d; 2c; 3b; 4d; 5a; 6d; 7d; 8c; 9a; 10d;

**Tuesday:** 1d; 2d; 3b; 4b; 5d; 6d; 7a, b, c, d; 8c; 9d; 10d;

**Wednesday:** 1b; 2b; 3c; 4d; 5d; 6c; 7a; 8b; 9a, b, c, d; 10d;

**Thursday:** 1d; 2 a, b, c, d; 3 a, b, c, d; 4d; 5 a, b, c, d; 6c; 7d; 8 a, b, c, d; 9 a, b, c, d; 10d;

**Friday:** 1a; 2a; 3d; 4c; 5d; 6c; 7b; 8d; 9d; 10b;

**Saturday:** 1a; 2d; 3a, b, c, d; 4d; 5a, 6b; 7a; 8a; 9b; 10a, b, c, d

# Notes

# MORE TITLES AVAILABLE IN THE 'IN A WEEK' SERIES

ADVANCED NEGOTIATION SKILLS • ASSERTIVENESS • BUSINESS ECONOMICS • COACHING • COPYWRITING • DECISION MAKING • DIFFICULT CONVERSATIONS • ECOMMERCE • FINANCE FOR NON-FINANCIAL MANAGERS • JOB INTERVIEWS • MANAGING STRESS AT WORK • MANAGING YOUR BOSS • MANAGING YOURSELF • MINDFULNESS AT WORK • NEGOTIATION SKILLS • NLP • PEOPLE SKILLS • PSYCHOMETRIC TESTING • SEO AND SEARCH MARKETING • SOCIAL MEDIA MARKETING • START YOUR OWN BUSINESS • STRATEGY • SUCCESSFUL SELLING • UNDERSTANDING AND INTERPRETING ACCOUNTS

For information about other titles in the 'In A Week' series, please visit www.teachyourself.co.uk

YOUR FASTEST ROUTE
TO SUCESS

LEARN IN A WEEK WHAT
THE EXPERTS LEARN
IN A LIFETIME

For information about other titles
in the 'In A Week' series, please visit
www.inaweek.co.uk